D1125358

University of Virginia

Charlottesville, Virginia

Written by Miriam Nicklin

Edited by Matt Hamman and Kimberly Moore

Layout by Adam Burns

*Additional contributions by Omid Gohari,
Christina Koshzow, Chris Mason, Joey Rahimi,
and Luke Skurman*

ISBN # 1-4274-0203-5
ISSN # 1552-1486

Last Updated 5/15/06

Special Thanks To: Babs Carryer, Andy Hannah, LaunchCyte, Tim O'Brien, Bob Sehlinger, Thomas Emerson, Andrew Skurman, Barbara Skurman, Bert Mann, Dave Lehman, Daniel Fayock, Chris Babyak, The Donald H. Jones Center for Entrepreneurship, Terry Slease, Jerry McGinnis, Bill Ecenberger, Idie McGinty, Kyle Russell, Jacque Zaremba, Larry Winderbaum, Roland Allen, Jon Reider, Team Evankovich, Lauren Varacalli, Abu Noaman, Mark Exler, Daniel Steinmeyer, Jared Cohon, Gabriela Oates, David Koegler, Glen Meakem, and the University of Virginia Bounce-Back Team.

College Prowler®
5001 Baum Blvd.
Suite 750
Pittsburgh, PA 15213

Phone: 1-800-290-2682
Fax: 1-800-772-4972
E-Mail: info@collegeprowler.com
Web Site: www.collegeprowler.com

How this all started...

When I was trying to find the perfect college, I used every resource that was available to me. I went online to visit school websites; I talked with my high school guidance counselor; I read book after book; I hired a private counselor. Sure, this was all very helpful, but nothing really told me what life was like at the schools I cared about. These sources weren't giving me enough information to be totally confident in my decision.

In all my research, there were only two ways to get the information I wanted.

The first was to physically visit the campuses and see if things were really how the brochures described them, but this was quite expensive and not always feasible. The second involved a missing ingredient: the students. Actually talking to a few students at those schools gave me a taste of the information that I needed so badly. The problem was that I wanted more but didn't have access to enough people.

In the end, I weighed my options and decided on a school that felt right and had a great academic reputation, but truth be told, the choice was still very much a crapshoot. I had done as much research as any other student, but was I 100 percent positive that I had picked the school of my dreams?

Absolutely not.

My dream in creating *College Prowler* was to build a resource that people can use with confidence. My own college search experience taught me the importance of gaining true insider insight; that's why the majority of this guide is composed of quotes from actual students. After all, shouldn't you hear about a school from the people who know it best?

I hope you enjoy reading this book as much as I've enjoyed putting it together. Tell me what you think when you get a chance. I'd love to hear your college selection stories.

Luke Skurman
CEO and Co-Founder
lukeskurman@collegeprowler.com

Welcome to College Prowler®

During the writing of College Prowler's guidebooks, we felt it was critical that our content was unbiased and unaffiliated with any college or university. We think it's important that our readers get honest information and a realistic impression of the student opinions on any campus—that's why if any aspect of a particular school is terrible, we (unlike a campus brochure) intend to publish it. While we do keep an eye out for the occasional extremist—the cheerleader or the cynic—we take pride in letting the students tell it like it is. We strive to create a book that's as representative as possible of each particular campus. Our books cover both the good and the bad, and whether the survey responses point to recurring trends or a variation in opinion, these sentiments are directly and proportionally expressed through our guides.

College Prowler guidebooks are in the hands of students throughout the entire process of their creation. Because you can't make student-written guides without the students, we have students at each campus who help write, randomly survey their peers, edit, layout, and perform accuracy checks on every book that we publish. From the very beginning, student writers gather the most up-to-date stats, facts, and inside information on their colleges. They fill each section with student quotes and summarize the findings in editorial reviews. In addition, each school receives a collection of letter grades (A through F) that reflect student opinion and help to represent contentment, prominence, or satisfaction for each of our 20 specific categories. Just as in grade school, the higher the mark the more content, more prominent, or more satisfied the students are with the particular category.

Once a book is written, additional students serve as editors and check for accuracy even more extensively. Our bounce-back team—a group of randomly selected students who have no involvement with the project—are asked to read over the material in order to help ensure that the book accurately expresses every aspect of the university and its students. This same process is applied to the 200-plus schools College Prowler currently covers. Each book is the result of endless student contributions, hundreds of pages of research and writing, and countless hours of hard work. All of this has led to the creation of a student information network that stretches across the nation to every school that we cover. It's no easy accomplishment, but it's the reason that our guides are such a great resource.

When reading our books and looking at our grades, keep in mind that every college is different and that the students who make up each school are not uniform—as a result, it is important to assess schools on a case-by-case basis. Because it's impossible to summarize an entire school with a single number or description, each book provides a dialogue, not a decision, that's made up of 20 different topics and hundreds of student quotes. In the end, we hope that this guide will serve as a valuable tool in your college selection process. Enjoy!

OMID GOHARI ◯ CHRISTINA KOSHZOW ◯ CHRIS MASON ◯ JOEY RAHIMI ◯ LUKE SKURMAN ◯
The College Prowler Team

Table of Contents

Introduction from the Author

Ever since ground was broken in the fall of 1817, the University of Virginia has remained tied to its roots, its history, and to founding father Thomas Jefferson's ideals. Jefferson once wrote: "knowledge is power, knowledge is safety, knowledge is happiness." Certainly these words of insight have been instilled into every soft red brick, every arch, and every student's mind at the University. The staff and students of UVA genuinely believe in Jefferson's principles and in the importance of intellect, but even more than that, Virginia students value one another's beliefs and cherish the ability to just relax, breathe, and take in all there is out there.

Coming into UVA, I must admit I was less than excited. I knew it was a great school academically, and I remember hearing the phrase "the Harvard of the South" multiple times from my father—who was also quick to point out how great a deal its in-state tuition was (and it really is). But there were things that scared me about the school: the notorious Greek life that seemed to infest the social scene, the enormous size of the student body, and the fact that my social security number was all that distinguished me from other students at summer orientation.

But not a month after graduation, I find that the longer I stay, the harder it is for me to leave. Charlottesville and UVA have their hooks in me. As I walk around Grounds and watch as the summer session students race to their classes, I wonder if they have had a chance to lie under the trees on the Lawn and look up towards the Rotunda; I wonder if they have had the chance to realize what a beautiful, inspiring place this is.

I wish you the best of luck in your college search, wherever you end up. I hope this book brings greater insight into the real experience at the University of Virginia, and, if you happen to someday find yourself walking around Jefferson's Grounds, I wish you some of the same affection and love that I have gradually gained for this place.

Miriam M. Nicklin, Author
University of Virginia

By the Numbers

General Information

University of Virginia
1740 University Ave
Charlottesville, VA 22903-2619

Control:
Public

Academic Calendar:
Semester

Religious Affiliation:
None

Founded:
1819

Web Site:
www.virginia.edu

Main Phone:
(434) 924-0311

Admissions Phone:
(434) 982-3200

Student Body

**Full-Time
Undergraduates:**
13,378

**Part-Time
Undergraduates**
751

**Total Male
Undergraduates:**
6,564

**Total Female
Undergraduates:**
7,565

Admissions

Overall Acceptance Rate:
39%

Early Decision Acceptance Rate:
39%

Regular Acceptance Rate:
39%

Total Applicants:
14,822

Total Acceptances:
5,760

Freshman Enrollment:
3,096

Yield (% of admitted students who actually enroll):
54%

Early Decision Available?
Yes

Early Decision One Deadline:
November 1

Early Action Available?
No

Early Decision One Notification:
Mailed by December 1

Regular Decision Deadline:
January 2

Regular Decision Notification:
Mailed by April 1

Must-Reply-By Date:
May 1

Applicants Placed on Waiting List:
3,017

Applicants Accepted from Waiting List:
1,809

Students Enrolled from Waiting List:
37

Transfer Applications Received:
2,210

Transfer Applications Accepted:
896

Transfer Students Enrolled:
578

Transfer Application Acceptance Rate:
65%

Common Application Accepted?
No

Supplemental Forms?
No

Admissions E-Mail:
undergrad-admission@virginia.edu

Admissions Web Site:
www.virginia.edu/schls.html

SAT I or ACT Required?
Both

→

**SAT I Range
(25th–75th Percentile):**
1230–1430

**SAT I Verbal Range
(25th–75th Percentile):**
610–710

**SAT I Math Range
(25th–75th Percentile):**
620–720

**SAT II Requirements for
all Schools:**
Math, Writing, and a subject of
your choice

Retention Rate:
97%

**Top 10% of
High School Class:**
84%

Application Fee:
$40

Financial Information

In-State Tuition:
$7,180

Out-of-State Tuition:
$24,100

Room and Board:
$6,389

Books and Supplies:
$1000

**Average Need-Based
Financial Aid Package
(including loans, work-study,
grants, and other sources):**
$14,135

**Students Who Applied for
Financial Aid:**
40%

Students Who Received Aid:
25%

Financial Aid Forms Deadline:
March 1 (for entering and
transfer students)

March 31 (for returning
students)

Financial Aid Phone:
(434) 982-6000

Financial Aid E-Mail:
faid@virginia.edu

Financial Aid Web Site:
www.virginia.edu/financialaid

Academics

The Lowdown On...
Academics

Degrees Awarded:
Bachelor
Master
Doctorate

Most Popular Majors:
12% Economics
10% Business
 9% Psychology
 8% English
 6% International Affairs

Undergraduate Schools:
Arts and Sciences
Architecture
Commerce
Education
Engineering
Nursing

Full-Time Faculty:
2,005

Faculty with Terminal Degree:
92%

Student-to-Faculty Ratio:
15:1

Average Course Load:
15 credits per semester

Graduation Rates:
Four-Year: 83%
Five-Year: 92%
Six-Year: 92%

Special Degree Options

Interdisciplinary studies (create your own major), double major, double minor

AP Test Score Requirements

Possible credit for scores of 4 or 5

IB Test Score Requirements

Possible credit for scores of 6 or 7

Sample Academic Clubs

Virginia Math Team, Technology Club, McIntire Entrepreneurs Group, Sigma Theta Delta International English Honor Society

Best Places to Study

Alderman or Clemons Libraries, the coffee shops on the Corner

Did You Know?

The Rotunda was designed by Thomas Jefferson after the Pantheon in Rome and is meant to symbolize the enlightened human mind. Jefferson chose this site at the head of campus to be a library, whereas most other 19th century universities often chose a chapel as their central feature.

UVA has **the highest graduation and retention rate** of any public college or university!

Students Speak Out On...
Academics

{ **"There are more excellent teachers
than bad teachers. Usually, you will get
a professor, but in some classes, you
end up with a graduate assistant (GA) or
teaching assistant (TA)."**

Q "During my time at UVA, I had a handful of the best,
as well as some of the most disinterested teachers I've
ever had. In my experience as a biology and psychology
double major, I found that the greatest challenge was the
way the courses were structured, and more specifically,
the class size of most of the courses. For courses within
my majors, it was not until my fourth and final year that I
had a class where the professor was close enough to me
that I did not need my glasses to make out his/her face.
I suppose that, in short, **I found most of my college
experience rather impersonal**. In order to overcome the
large class sizes and truly get to know a professor, one
has to expend a good deal of energy going to extra office
hours, and staying after class. As a result of this dynamic,
some of my more influential teacher-student relationships
at UVA were with TAs."

Q "There are bad and there are good teachers. The majority
of teachers I have interacted with are friendly and do care
whether or not you are actually learning. You get to know
them better in smaller classes; however, many smaller
classes are taught by grad students. Those classes are less
desirable. **I've heard horror stories of teachers/grad
students who spoke very little English**, but I never had
the misfortune of being in one of their classes."

Q "Most of the classes I took at UVA were very interesting. **The professors were enthusiastic** and really knew their stuff. Some of my classes, on the other hand, were almost always boring and badly taught. The professors did not seem to be in touch with the students at all, and they were impossible to reach outside of class. Many of them did not know the subject matter of the class at all. One professor rarely even showed up for class."

Q "It all depends. Some of the teachers are a real snooze, and others are really fantastic. Some of them (with tenure) know they're not going anywhere, so **they don't really care about their students.**"

Q "You have to go out of your way to **make sure your professors know you.**"

Q "**Most of UVA's teachers are distinguished**, but just because they are very educated doesn't mean they're good teachers."

Q "**Some of the unknown teachers teach some of the best classes** I have ever had. I don't think I missed a thing by not taking classes with some of the well-known professors."

Q "It depends on what your major is, the type of classes you're taking, and your own academic ability. It's extremely relative. I'm a second-year major in the humanities. At all costs (unless it's mandated), **avoid 101 courses.** Chemistry, calculus, economics, and statistics are quite challenging, so beware."

Q "You'll have some lectures taught by professors, and smaller ones taught by grad students who are getting their PhDs. **All the lectures I had this year were really good, on the whole.**"

Q "The teachers here are really great. When you are still young, **most classes will be large lectures**, and as you declare a major, they get smaller. All professors have office hours, and if you go to them, you will get to know your teachers even more. I have yet to be disappointed by any of my teachers. They all seem to be really nice."

Q "The TAs are really helpful. I find that I've had better relationships with them than some professors, because every large lecture is also broken into a small discussion section with the TA. During the smaller discussion sections is where **you'll get more productive, interactive learning**."

The College Prowler Take On...
Academics

Most students agree that the professors at UVA are outstanding, qualified, brilliant, passionate men and women. As expected, there are occasional complaints about class structure, material, and size, as well as some unfortunate cases of disinterested teachers. The quality and interest level of classes and professors vary throughout the different schools and departments at UVA. For the most part, students find that classes and professors in the College of Arts and Sciences (particularly the English, drama, history, and psychology departments) are more liberal and interesting. Some of the more technical, scientific courses and schools (biology or engineering, for example) can be a necessary burden, even for students specializing in those fields.

Though the best professors tend to only teach upperclassmen, be patient. Learn from your TA in the meantime—even though it may be disappointing and frustrating at times. Remember that TAs are more accessible, younger, and often more enthusiastic about the classes they're working with; you can use this to your advantage and get more out of your learning experience. In general, as long as you are interested in developing a relationship with some of your teachers, whether they be TAs or professors, you will no doubt excel academically at Virginia.

The College Prowler® Grade on

Academics: A-

A high Academics grade generally indicates that professors are knowledgeable, accessible, and genuinely interested in their students' welfare. Other determining factors include class size, how well professors communicate, and whether or not classes are engaging.

Local Atmosphere

The Lowdown On...
Local Atmosphere

Region:
South

City, State:
Charlottesville, VA

Setting:
Small college town

Distance from Washington DC:
2 hours, 30 minutes

Distance from Richmond, VA:
1 hour, 30 minutes

Points of Interest:
Beaver Creek
The Blue Ridge Mountains
The Downtown Mall
The Farmer's Market
The James River
Mince Springs
Monticello

Closest Shopping Malls:

The Barracks Shopping Center
1117 Emmet St.
Charlottesville,VA 22903
(434) 977-0100

The Downtown Mall
600 College Dr.
Charlottesville, VA 22902
(434) 977-1783

Fashion Square Mall
1600 Rio Rd. E
Charlottesville, VA 22901
(434) 973-9331

Closest Movie Theaters:

Carmike 6 Theater
1803 Seminole Trail
Charlottesville, VA 22901
(434) 973-4294

Downtown Mall 6
200 W. Main St.
Charlottesville, VA 22902
(434) 979-7857

The Jefferson Theater
110 E Main St.
Charlottesville, VA 22902
(434) 295-3321

Major Sports Teams:

None, just the UVA
sports teams

City Web Sites

www.charlottesvilletourism.org
www.charlottesvilleguide.com

Did You Know?

5 Fun Facts about Charlottesville:

- Charlottesville is **the home of the Dave Matthews Band**—both where they started and where they live now (when they're not out on tour).

- The Virginia Film Festival comes to Charlottesville every October and is hosted by the University, **bringing with it famous actors, directors, producers, and screenwriters**. In recent years, Sigourney Weaver, Anthony Hopkins, Nicolas Cage, Roger Ebert, and Sissy Spacek have all taken part in the festival.

- During the summer months, **there is a Farmer's Market** that takes place every Saturday morning right next to the Downtown Mall.

- Every March Charlottesville hosts the Virginia Festival of the Book that attracts many brilliant writers and poets and **further inspires the artistic community**.

- Monticello, **the hilltop home of Thomas Jefferson**, is not only known for its amazing architecture, but also for the former president's many showcased inventions.

Famous Charlottesville Residents:

Katie Couric

John Grisham

Thomas Jefferson

Jessica Lange

Dave Matthews (and his band)

Sam Shepherd

Sissy Spacek

Students Speak Out On...
Local Atmosphere

"There's a lot to visit in C-ville. The places I would recommend are the Downtown Mall, Humpback Rock, Beaver Creek, Crabtree Falls, Monticello, and the Rotunda."

Q "Charlottesville has a small-town feel, which at times is wonderful and relaxing, and at other times is stifling and insulating. There is a community college nearby called Piedmont, although I wouldn't say this has a huge impact on the University community. Overall, I always thought of Charlottesville as made up of college kids (mostly affluent and from other cities), the professors and their families, the ex-hippies who landed in Charlottesville because it has a liberal-friendly feel, and all the other people affectionately referred to by the college kids as 'townies.' Definitely find time to visit the Downtown Mall. There is a free trolley from the Corner and Grounds. **The Downtown Mall is a great place to see a movie**, grab some dinner, or just walk around."

Q "There are no other universities really, although some commute to Piedmont. **The town is really nice in areas that are generally populated with University students**, such as the Corner, Barracks Road, and Downtown Mall. However, there are some sections of town that you definitely want to stay away from. So if you are wandering around, and all of a sudden it looks like you are in Compton, turn around and go back the way you came."

Q "**Townies don't like us**. We don't like townies. There's a big rivalry."

Q "There's Piedmont Community College nearby. There isn't a lot of mixing of the two schools, though. I think Charlottesville is a college town when you're in college, but **there's a really rich community outside of UVA**. There are live arts, theaters, restaurants, wineries, estates, and more rich-people stuff."

Q "Go to the parks, the creeks, and the lakes. Specifically, go to Humpback Rock (off of Skyline Drive in the Blue Ridge Mountains), Walnut Creek, Mince Springs, and Beaver Creek. **There are some bad neighborhoods to stay away from, especially at night**—anything past 14th Street going away from Grounds."

Q "It's a close-knit community, especially the Corner district. **Just because it's not a huge district doesn't mean it isn't fun**. It's cool because you run into friends all the time and have a good time, but then, the Charlottesville community, overall, has a lot of tension with UVA."

Q "I think Charlottesville is a much divided community. UVA students think they are in their own little worlds. But Charlottesville has a lot to offer. **Try to go to events that are not alcohol-related**: I'd check out anything on the Downtown Mall, the Virginia Art Museum, or elsewhere."

Q "There's a community college, but **the atmosphere is mostly like the school** until you get into downtown or the country; then, it's pretty family-oriented and artsy."

Q "From musical UVA concerts, to professional singers, to famous speakers, to going to downtown Charlottesville, movies, ice-skating, and tons of restaurants; there is **never a lack of things to do**."

Q "Charlottesville is nice. The mountains are nearby, and it's **a liberal town**. It's close to DC, so internships are not far off."

Q "It's a great social scene. Everyone is always finding fun new things to do in Charlottesville. There are outdoor activities at your fingertips, and you can always run to the mall if you are desperate for the newest thing at Express. **People are always going out, making new friends, and visiting pubs on the Corner.**"

Q "**Charlottesville is a cute little town that's dominated by the University.** There's really nothing to avoid, and there's a fair amount of stuff to visit, like Monticello and the mountains."

Q "I love Charlottesville; it's a real college town. **JMU and Virginia Tech kids visit a lot.** The downtown area is really cute and fun, and there is decent shopping."

The College Prowler Take On...
Local Atmosphere

Charlottesville has a unique, artistic, natural feel to it. It is surrounded by the beautiful hills and mountains of the Blue Ridge, which, alone, have much to offer—from hiking and picnicking, to a simple stroll along Skyline Drive. There are plenty of lakes and ponds just outside of town where students like to lie out and cool off in the summer and spring. The real cultural center of Charlottesville is mainly in and around the Downtown Mall, where there are many art galleries, music clubs, bookstores, and theaters. There is a great artistic tradition in Charlottesville. Many writers, musicians, and artists reside and work in and around the town which, no doubt, inspires them.

Despite all there is to do and see in Charlottesville, many students neglect to recognize the town's rich culture and numerous opportunities. UVA students sometimes arrogantly forget that they are in the greater Charlottesville community and get too wrapped up in being a part of the University. As a result, there seems to be quite a bit of tension between students and locals. The University certainly makes up a large part of Charlottesville, and many students take this as an excuse not to explore the area. Charlottesville remains a vibrant, intellectual, but also laid-back town. Although it can seem stifling at times, the area has more than enough for you to discover over your four years of college. If you're willing to be creative and explore new places, there's a lot to be found.

B

The College Prowler® Grade on

Local Atmosphere: B

A high Local Atmosphere grade indicates that the area surrounding campus is safe and scenic. Other factors include nearby attractions, proximity to other schools, and the town's attitude toward students.

Safety & Security

The Lowdown On...
Safety & Security

Number of UVA Police Officers:

190 (60 UVA police, 130 security staff)

www.virginia.edu/uvapolice

Health Center Office Hours:

Monday–Friday
8 a.m.–5 p.m.,
Saturday 8:30 a.m.–12 p.m.

Phone Numbers:

UVA Police Crime Prevention:
(434) 924-8845

Health System
Emergency Room:
(434) 924-2231

Elson Student Health Center:
(434) 924-5362

Sexual Assault Resource
Agency (SARA):
(434) 977-7273

Sexual Assault Education
coordinator:
(434) 982-2774

911 (emergencies)
(434) 924-7166

Safety Services

Blue-light phones

Self-defense classes

Safety information

Escort service (Shuttle runs from 8 p.m.–7 a.m., (434) 242-1122)

Lighted Pathway System (emergency phones, video cameras, and bright overhead lighting)

Health Services

www.virginia.edu/studenthealth

Phone Numbers

Main Number: (434) 924-5362

Administration: (434) 924-5471

After Hours (emergency clinician on call): (434) 972-7004

Allergy Clinic: (434) 924-1522

Billing Questions: (434) 243-2794

Counseling and Psychological Services (CAPS): (434) 924-5556

Cold Study/Flu Study: (434) 924-2371

General Medicine (Appointments): (434) 982-3915

Gynecology (Appointments): (434) 924-5362

Health Promotion: (434) 924-1509

Learning Needs and Evaluation Center (LNEC): (434) 243-5181 or (434) 243-5180

Medical Records: (434) 924-1525

Nutritional Counseling: (434) 924-1509

Pharmacy: (434) 924-1544

Student Health Insurance Plan & Referrals: (434) 243-2702

UVA Hospital Emergency Department: (434) 924-2231

Did You Know?

In 2005, the following crimes were reported on UVA Grounds:

Aggravated Assault: 9

Arson: 4

Burglary: 74

Forcible Sex Offenses: 3

Hate Crimes/Prejudice: 1 (race-related)

Manslaughter: 0

Motor Vehicle Theft: 2

Murder/Non-Negligent Manslaughter: 0

Non-Forcible Sex Offenses: 3

Robbery: 4

Students Speak Out On...
Safety & Security

> **"I've always felt really safe here. I think most other students do, too. A lot of being safe is just using common sense."**

Q "I've never really felt unsafe on grounds, but not a year goes by that there isn't talk of someone getting hurt. **There is at least one rape per year**. In the grand scheme of things, that's really not that many, and on any given night, your chances are good, but it still happens."

Q "**UVA is pretty safe since it's in a small town**. There is a serial rapist on the loose, though."

Q "I usually feel safe on campus, because there are generally **lots of other students nearby**; however, after working as a volunteer with a rape-crisis hotline, I know there are many incidents that occur even on what feels like a safe campus."

Q "I always felt very safe when I was at UVA—almost too safe. I became naive almost, like nothing could ever happen to me. **I always see cops around**, and blue-light emergency phones are all over."

Q "Coming from a guy, I've never had any problems walking alone at night, but **the recent assault and battery incidents have caused me to worry** about my female friends. I always make sure after parties that they have an escort home."

Q "Security is pretty good here. Personally, I have never had any problems with things getting stolen, and I've never had anyone follow me. **There are security phones all over campus**, and you can always find a police officer when you need one. So I'd say that there are no problems in that area."

Q "Security is great because not only do we have our own police department, but we also have officers who patrol the grounds on a frequent basis. In addition, we have **student escorts that transport students at night**, so you don't have to worry about walking alone."

Q "The security is great at Virginia. We have our own Virginia police. If you need a ride home from somewhere on the campus at night, **you can dial UVA security and they will give you a ride home**. I've personally never heard of any security problems at the campus."

Q "You can check out cell phones from the library. They have a link to 911 on them, and you can use them if you're going to walk home and either don't feel safe or don't want to call an escort. **All of the University's police officers carry guns and are fully trained** (they're not just security guards). Personally, I have never, ever felt scared here, and many girls walk around by themselves at all hours of the night. There is very little crime, most likely due to our honor system which holds much water here."

Q "Security and safety are, for the most part, good, but you still should be careful (don't walk alone at night). There are buses and an escort service, which is a free ride that you can call to safely take you where you need to go. And campus police are all over, **mostly making sure everyone is getting home okay**."

Q **"The Virginia campus is one of the safest in the nation**.
There are not many things that call for campus police
involvement, and if anything does require their assistance,
they understand that we are college students and try to
help us out more than punish us."

Q "**On the whole, Virginia is very safe**; however, there are
a few exceptions, as with almost all places in the world. I
think that safety awareness is pretty high here and that the
students really do look out for one another."

The College Prowler Take On...
Safety & Security

Most students at UVA feel pretty safe. The UVA police and security force is quite a noticeable presence on grounds—in addition to the school's 90 police officers, there is a staff of about 130 security workers. Standard campus security services are offered at UVA (blue-light phones, escort services), but the best tools are common sense and simply being aware. If there's one flaw in the security at UVA, it's that students sometimes don't understand the importance of looking out for safety. As one student said, it's easy to feel "almost too safe." On campus and in parts of Charlottesville, life can seem over-insulated at times, and when tragedies happen, it comes as a shock to many.

As with any college, UVA can be unsafe if you're not looking out for yourself. Sexual assaults have become a bigger problem over the last few years, particularly in off-grounds housing areas where it is more difficult for campus police to monitor activity. For the most part, however, you'll have little to worry about during your time at the University. Students are advised to simply use common sense and stay informed of what's going on around the grounds.

B+

The College Prowler® Grade on

Safety & Security: B+

A high grade in Safety & Security means that students generally feel safe, campus police are visible, blue-light phones and escort services are readily available, and safety precautions are not overly necessary.

Computers

The Lowdown On...
Computers

High-Speed Network?
Yes

Wireless Network?
Yes

Number of Computers:
1,859

Number of Labs:
11

Operating Systems:
Mac
PC
Unix

Discounted Software

None

Free Software

Many applications are available to students and staff through ITC; check online for an updated list: *www.itc.virginia.edu/desktop/central*

24-Hour Labs

Cocke Hall, Clemons Library, and the chemistry building are just some of the labs open 24 hours.

Charge to Print?

Yes. Eight cents per sheet for black-and-white, 60 cents per sheet for color; printing can only be done using your Cavalier Advantage account (with your UVA student ID).

Did You Know?

UVA is one of the few schools **with almost 100 percent wireless coverage**. Despite UVA's top-notch computer facilities, more than 85 percent of students bring their own computers to school.

Students Speak Out On...
Computers

{ **"I had my own computer and preferred to use it instead of the computer labs. Generally, the computer labs are really nice for simple things like word processing. The network is fast, too."**

Q "I did not find the computer labs to be very crowded whenever I used them. Sometimes, there was a wait of a few minutes to get a computer. Printing in the computer labs seems to be the bigger problem, as there were always back-ups at the printers. If you have your own computer, I would definitely recommend bringing it. **In the dorms there is free Internet access, and it is fast**. If you move off grounds, you are on your own, but it still seems like having a computer would be an asset just due to the amount of assignments that are now requested to be typed."

Q **"During the semester everyone goes to the computer lab between classes to check their e-mail**, so it is very busy then. Generally, I think it is safe to say you could always find a computer somewhere to work on a paper or project, if you didn't have one of your own, but it makes life so much easier to have your own. There is Ethernet in all the rooms if you live on grounds, and there are a bunch of options if you live off grounds, as well, ranging from $20 a month for dial-up and $40–$50 for DSL."

www.collegeprowler.com

COMPUTERS | 27

Q "**UVA has a great wireless network** covering almost the whole campus, so if you have a wireless Ethernet card in your laptop, you can get onto the network almost anywhere in UVA. So you could write your papers on the lawn, at your desk, in the library, or anywhere. Unfortunately, UVA hasn't done a good job of promoting this, so none of the students know that they can take advantage of it. Also, it's very difficult to get onto the network at first because the workers at ITC (the on-grounds technical help desk) are inefficient at helping students get accounts."

Q "You should bring your own computer, and make sure you have a printer, since **you have to pay to print** in the labs now."

Q "During my four years here, **I never needed my own computer**. Labs are only crowded between classes and right before midterms and finals. You never have to wait that long."

Q "I think it's a big convenience to have your own computer, but not a necessity. **I think you can get by using friends' computers or the labs**, but if you want to print, make sure you have money to do so."

Q "**Definitely bring your own computer**! They have computers, but it's just a lot easier to do all your work at home in your room."

Q "You don't need a computer, but I would get one if you can afford it. If not, there are more than enough on the Grounds. Virginia has one of the best computer-based campuses in the United States. Everything from registration to grades is online. **Most of my class notes were posted before lecture**, so I could print them and then take notes on them. That was nice. You will print all class material from the Web."

Q "Everything is wired, and the Internet is so fast. I know many people who do not bring computers because there are computer labs in nearly every building with the fast Internet. There are also labs near the dorms. On the other hand, due to this age of technology, many people do bring computers. **All the rooms are wired**."

Q "**We have unlimited access to computers**. We have computer labs in every area, from the dormitories to the libraries. You can also check out laptops at the library, if need be. I would bring a laptop over a huge computer, but that's my personal opinion. You can also purchase a computer through school. I purchased mine through Virginia, and all I had to do was basically turn it on because all the necessary software and hardware were already installed on the computer. They also will put your computer in your dorm room, and it will be waiting for you when you arrive on grounds."

Q "You don't have to bring a computer, as there are many **labs that are never crowded**. Regardless, it may be a good idea to have one."

Q "The network in the dorms is fast, and the computer labs are abundant, so **finding a free computer isn't hard**."

Q "Computers are abundant; there are some in the dorms. **Only on finals week would I say that they are crowded**."

Q "It's always better to bring your own computer, but there are **a lot of computer labs that are not crowded**."

The College Prowler Take On...
Computers

Generally, students find that the UVA computer system and labs are well-equipped and really quite efficient. However, most agree that despite the excellent computer facilities and their convenience, it is much easier to have your own computer. Many students find that the labs get too crowded between classes, as well as during midterms and finals. Additionally, the school's extensive wireless network makes having your own laptop a huge advantage—you can access the Internet from nearly anywhere on campus once you have your account set up. The biggest complaint these days seems to be the nagging pay-for-print policy. Following state budget cuts, the administration had to implement this rule. Students were upset by the new situation–especially those with classes that rely almost entirely on Internet readings or presentations that need to be printed out. If you're doing a lot of word processing or printing, it may be more cost-effective to bring your own computer and printer. The labs and computer system are all excellent, but the printing has become a huge pain between costs and long queue back-ups.

Overall, technology at UVA more than meets the needs of the student body, and you'll be able to survive if you can't bring your own computer. To get the best experience at the University, however, consider both a laptop (with wireless access) and your own printer.

B-

The College Prowler® Grade on

Computers: B-

A high grade in Computers designates that computer labs are available, the computer network is easily accessible, and the campus' computing technology is up-to-date.

Facilities

The Lowdown On...
Facilities

Student Center:
Newcomb Hall

Athletic Center:
UVA has multiple gyms and athletic facilities, including the AFC, Memorial Gym, North Grounds, and Slaughter Gym.

Campus Size:
1,682 acres

Libraries:
Alderman
Clemons
Four other departmental libraries

Popular Places to Chill:
The Lawn during nice weather
The Corner
Clemons Library

What Is There to Do on Campus?

Work out in the AFC (Aquatic Fitness Center) or any other gym (Memorial Gym, North Grounds, Slaughter Gym); take a dip in the hot tub or rest up in the sauna on the ground floor of the AFC; check out a play in Culbreth Theater, or see a relatively recent movie playing in the basement of Newcomb Hall; have coffee in the library at Greenberry's, or a smoothie with friends in the PAV.

Movie Theater on Campus?

Yes, Newcomb Hall Theater (located in the basement of Newcomb Hall).

Bowling on Campus?

No

Bar on Campus?

No, there are bars just off the grounds, however.

Coffeehouse on Campus?

Yes, there's a Greenberry's in Alderman Library and the Bookstore. There are also several snack places that are sure to have coffee: the PAV, the Bakery, and the Castle.

Favorite Things to Do

UVA students have been known to work out, lie on the lawn, grab a meal with friends, walk to a bar off campus, and see a movie in Newcomb all in a span of one day!

Students Speak Out On...
Facilities

{ **"The AFC is great—though I wish the pool was open more. I constantly wanted to swim when the pool wasn't open. In terms of fitness equipment, UVA is great."**

Q "UVA really cares about its athletes and sports-fan ticket holders. The athletic facilities are top-notch and I understand that a new basketball arena is even in the works. The computers in the labs are also nice, and the student center, Newcomb Hall, is fine, too. While all these facilities are nice, **the administration shows its bias toward athletics at UVA**, as students watch privileges like free and unlimited printing in the computer labs go down the tubes in the course of the same year in which ground is broken for the new basketball arena."

Q "The facilities depend on which school you are in. The engineering school's facilities (such as the library and computer labs) are old, dirty, uncomfortable, and falling apart. Most of the classrooms are in the basement with no windows, and students must sit in cramped seating. **They recently constructed a new library**, though, and it's supposed to be very high-tech and comfortable for students to use. The law school facilities, on the other hand, are awesome—very high-tech, clean, and comfortable."

Q "Right now, the facilities are adequate, but in the next several years, you're basically gonna have a whole new UVA. The school is **implementing a wide range of new construction, additions, and renovations** that will make the school even better than it is."

Q "**All of the facilities at Virginia are state-of-the-art** and frequently undergo renovation in order to keep them running well."

Q "Everyone works out, so the gyms are great. **There are also plenty of computers with Internet and e-mail.**"

Q "**Facilities are nice**, and new buildings are being built, like a new parking garage, new basketball stadium, and other things like that."

Q "**There are new facilities, as well as old ones**, and there are a lot of new ones being built."

Q "Athletic facilities are pretty good. The computer labs are a little lacking. **We didn't really have what I would call a student center before, but now we do.**"

Q "**Facilities are state-of-the-art**, including our gym, and especially the Aquatic Fitness Center."

Q "When it comes to facilities, Virginia has the best around. The gyms are great and have the most modern and safe equipment. There are more computer labs than I can count, and the libraries are renowned. **All athletic events are free to students and so much fun**—I love all the football games!"

Q "There are great workout areas; we have three gyms. The libraries are really nice, too. **They have every book we could possibly need.**"

Q "**The AFC is really nice**, but it tends to be really busy."

Q "The student center used to just consist of Newcomb Theater and a sketchy game room that no one ever used, but now, we have a nice student-faculty center with dining and very modern facilities. The athletic facilities are really nice, too. **The school is under-funded**."

The College Prowler Take On...
Facilities

Students agree that the athletic facilities (especially the Aquatic and Fitness Center) are superb. There always seem to be some sort of renovations going on; they are currently working on construction of several new facilities, and they're renovating many older ones. However, despite the excellent gyms and new athletic-and fitness-oriented projects, UVA sometimes neglects other parts of the campus. Some students will complain about the condition of labs and classrooms within the various colleges; though, complaints about the lack of a proper student center have finally ceased in recent years with the renovation of the new Newcomb Hall.

UVA makes sure to take care of every sort of athletic need; it is unfortunate that it does not do the same for its arts. While there is certainly a theater (two, in fact, when counting the black box), a photo lab, and a studio, the University still lacks a real arts center (though there is a new one in the works). Considering the fact that UVA is a rather under-funded public university, it does do quite well with what it has. For the most part, computer labs and classrooms are very nice and well-equipped, and the constant construction around campus shows signs of progress.

The College Prowler® Grade on
Facilities: B

A high Facilities grade indicates that the campus is aesthetically pleasing and well-maintained; facilities are state-of-the-art, and libraries are exceptional. Other determining factors include the quality of both athletic and student centers and an abundance of things to do on campus.

Campus Dining

The Lowdown On...
Campus Dining

Freshman Meal Plan Requirement?

Yes

Meal Plan Average Cost:

$1,550

Places to Grab a Bite with Your Meal Plan:

Alderman Café

Food: Coffee, tea, baked goods, bagels

Location: Alderman Library, fourth floor

Hours: Monday–Thursday 8 a.m.–11 p.m.,
Friday 8 a.m.–5 p.m.,
Saturday 12 p.m.–6 p.m.,
Sunday 1 p.m.–11 p.m.

The Bakery

Food: Coffee, bagels, breads, pastries, salads, soups

Location: Newcomb Hall, ground floor

Hours: Monday–Thursday 8 a.m.–5:30 p.m., Friday 8 a.m.–4 p.m., Sunday 11 a.m.–5 p.m.

C3 at Lambeth

Food: Snacks, chips, beverages

Location: Lambeth Field apartment complex

Hours: Monday–Friday 5 p.m.–12 a.m., Saturday–Sunday 12 p.m.–12 a.m.

C3 at Newcomb

Food: Snacks, chips, beverages

Location: Newcomb Hall

Hours: Monday–Friday 8 p.m.–11 p.m., Saturday closed, Sunday 3 p.m.–11 p.m.

C3 at Runk

Food: Snacks, chips, beverages

Location: Hereford College

Hours: Daily 4 p.m.–12 a.m.

The Castle

Food: Ben & Jerry's Ice Cream (ice cream), Grille Works (grilled hamburgers, chicken, fries, philly sandwiches and breakfast items), Kettle Classics Soup Station (soups, beverages, breads), Montague's Deli (sandwiches)

Location: Bonnycastle Dorm, ground floor

Hours: Monday–Thursday 8:30 a.m.–2 a.m., Friday 8:30 a.m.–3 p.m., Sunday 4 p.m.–2 a.m.

The Crossroads

Food: Pao's Panini (specialty sandwiches), Sbarro's (pizza, Italian), The Stoplight Grill (burgers, fries)

Location: West Campus

Hours: Monday–Thursday 8 a.m.–1 a.m., Friday 8 a.m.–2 a.m., Saturday 3 p.m.–2 a.m., Sunday 3 p.m.–12 a.m.

Fine Arts Lounge

Food: Breakfast biscuits, bagels, pastries, coffee, soup, deli sandwiches

Location: Fiske-Kimball Fine Arts Library, ground floor

Hours: Monday–Thursday 8:30 a.m.–4 p.m., Friday 8:30 a.m.–2 p.m.

Java City

Food: Coffee, pastries

Location: UVA Bookstore

Hours: Monday–Friday
8:30 a.m.–6 p.m.,
Saturday 11 a.m.–6 p.m.

Language Houses

Food: Dinner variety

Location: The French House,
Spanish House, Shea House

Hours: Monday–Thursday
5:30 p.m.–7:30 p.m.

The Market at Lambeth

Location: Lambeth Dorms

Food: Groceries, candy

Hours: Monday–Friday,
5 p.m.–12 a.m., Saturday–
Sunday 12 p.m.–12 a.m.

Newcomb Hall

Food: Cafeteria-style

Location: Central Grounds

Hours: Monday–Thursday
Breakfast 7 a.m.–10:15 a.m.
Lunch 10:45 a.m.–2:15 p.m.
Snack bar 2:15 p.m.–4 p.m.
Dinner 5 p.m.–8 p.m.

Friday 7 a.m.–10:15 a.m.,
10:45 a.m.–2:15 p.m.

Saturday 10 a.m.–2 p.m.

Sunday 10 a.m.–2 p.m.,
5 p.m.–8 p.m.

Observatory Hill

Food: Cafeteria-style

Location: Next to the
first-year dorms

Hours: Monday–Friday
7 a.m.–10:15 a.m.,
10:45 a.m.–2 p.m.,
2 p.m.–4 p.m.,
5 p.m.–8 p.m.

Saturday–Sunday
10 a.m.–2 p.m., 2 p.m.–
4 p.m., 5 p.m.–8 p.m.

Pavilion XI

Location: Newcomb Hall,
Ground Floor

Food: Chick-fil-A (chicken
sandwiches, waffle fries),
Cranberry Farms (turkey,
cranberry sauce, mashed
potatoes), Freshens
(smoothies, ice cream,
yogurt), Montague's Deli
(made-to-order deli)

Hours: Monday–Thursday
10 a.m.– p.m., Friday
8 a.m.–8 p.m., Saturday
12 p.m.–8 p.m.

Poolside Café

Location: Aquatic
Fitness Center

Food: Smoothies,
sandwiches, salads

Hours: Monday–Thursday
7:30 a.m.–9 p.m.,
Friday 7:30 a.m.–8 p.m,
Saturday–Sunday closed

Runk Hall

Food: Cafeteria-style

Location: Hereford College

Hours: Monday–Friday
Breakfast 7 a.m.–10:15 am
Continental Breakfast
10:15 a.m.–10:40 a.m.
Lunch 10:45 a.m.–2:15 p.m.
Dinner 5 p.m.–8 p.m.

Saturday–Sunday
10 a.m.–2 p.m.
5 p.m.–8 p.m.

Sidley, Austin, Brown, and Wood Cafè

Food: Bene Pizzeria (pizza, calzones), Grille Works (burgers, fries), Kettle Classics (soups, breads) World's Fare (international hot entrees, sides), Montague's Deli (specialty sandwiches)

Location: Student Faculty Center, 1st floor

Hours: Monday–Friday
8 a.m.–2 p.m., Saturday–Sunday closed

West Range Cafè

Food: Coffee, smoothies

Location: Next to Garrett Hall

Hours: Monday–Thursday
8 a.m.–6 p.m.,
Friday 8 a.m.–3 p.m.

Student Favorites:

Greenberry's (Alderman Café)

Pavillion XI

24-Hour On-Campus Eating:

No

Did You Know?

With your meal plan you get a certain amount of Plus Dollars, which allow you to purchase food at all the on-campus eateries (the regular meal plan only allows you to go to one of the three dining halls on grounds). Be sure to use all of these Plus Dollars up by the end of the academic year, as **you will not get them back**.

Students Speak Out On...
Campus Dining

{ **"Dining hall food is dining hall food, for the most part. Some of the food they serve is really sub-par, but the dining halls all have some sort of ethnic/alternative meal station, which is usually pretty good."**

Q "The food isn't that good. **Breakfast at Newcomb is the best.**"

Q "It's not horrible. You can find decent stuff. **There's always salad stuff.** The problem is they serve the same thing over and over again."

Q "I love the dining hall! **I had a meal plan for all four years.** Some days are definitely better than others, but I could always find something to eat—though, maybe not always the healthiest. Chick-fil-A was so clutch."

Q "The food on campus is something you should get away from as soon as you possibly can. It doesn't seem bad at first, but night after night of eating the same generic food gets old fast. **If you are a vegetarian or vegan, you are bound to have an even harder time.** As a vegetarian, I often found myself frustrated with the options and unable to put together a balanced meal, ending up with cereal for dinner many nights."

Q "**The dining halls suck.** After my first year, I never ever went back."

Q "UVA dining **leaves a lot to be desired**. Compared to other schools, UVA doesn't really have a wide assortment of choices. UVA needs more fast food on grounds."

Q "Since I was a freshman this past year, I mostly ate on campus. **It is pretty good**; there is a lot of variety."

Q "On grounds, dining halls are pretty standard, but the food quality is mostly good, and there's a large variety. There's also the Corner meal plan that allows you to eat at certain restaurants using this card that's like a credit card exclusively for Virginia students, I highly recommend it. Oh, and **the PAV is a place on Grounds that you pay for with Plus Dollars** (included in a standard meal plan) or regular money, or Cavalier Advantage, which is like the Corner meal plan except it's for on-grounds stuff. It all makes more sense once you get here."

Q "I like cafeteria food, although some people don't feel the same way. It is all you can eat, and I go by this rule: **take twice as much as you can eat**, because halfway through something, you'll decide you don't like it anymore and move on to something else. That way, half of two sandwiches make a whole."

Q "**The salad bars are good** and vegetarian friendly."

Q "**The food is okay**. We also have Plus Dollars that you can use at places like the PAV, which has Chick-fil-A and other stuff on grounds."

Q "Food is great—well, **it depends on what you like**. If you are not a fan of the dining halls (O-Hill, Newcomb, Runk) you can hit up the Treehouse (Pizza Hut and the Grill) or the Pavilion (Chick-fil-A, Cranberry Farms, Smoothie King, Bene Pizza, and the Bagel shop)."

Q "On grounds, where all freshmen eat, it is definitely not bad at all; there are a lot of options for even the most picky eaters. **The best dining halls are O-Hill and Newcomb**."

Q "Campus food is no good. As usual, **it's a cafeteria, so it can't be helped**, but they do have some nice places to eat on campus. They're expensive though."

Q "**It depends on where you live**. Newcomb Hall is pretty good, and Runk is the worst."

Q "As a first-year student, you will be required to buy a meal plan. The dining halls serve really good food—at least, Runk and Newcomb do; O-hill is not so good. **There are a ton of snack places on campus**."

The College Prowler Take On...
Campus Dining

Most students find the on-grounds dining to be pretty standard, as far as cafeteria food goes. Some say that they love the dining halls, but these students are few and far between. The salad, wrap, cereal, and ethnic/alternative food stations are normally pretty reliable, in that everyone can probably find something to eat there. The biggest complaint seems to be that the food is always the same. It is sometimes difficult for vegetarians and vegans to find something that suits their needs. After you tire of the dining hall, you can use Plus Dollars, CAV advantage, or cash in the PAV, bakery, the Castle, or any other on-grounds food facility. Though the food in these places is much better than the dining hall routine and predictability, it is, for the most part, not the healthiest.

You won't go hungry at UVA, even if you won't be eating as well as you did at home. Dining hall food is what it is—unchanging, bland, but filling. Many students enjoy Sunday brunches, with a make-your-own omelet station and all sorts of other fatty foods to soak up the alcohol from the night before. The PAV and the bakery, located on the ground floor of Newcomb Hall, are always pleasant breaks from the cafeteria. Despite the standard repetition, the dining hall does offer a good number of options, as well as the opportunity to chat with friends and have lively group meals.

The College Prowler® Grade on

Campus Dining: C-

Our grade on Campus Dining addresses the quality of both school-owned dining halls and independent on-campus restaurants as well as the price, availability, and variety of food.

Off-Campus Dining

The Lowdown On...
Off-Campus Dining

Restaurant Prowler:
Popular Places to Eat!

Amigos Inc
Food: Mexican

1863 Seminole Rd.

(434) 973-9301

Cool Features: On Wednesday nights enjoy $2.50 margaritas.

Price: $5–$7 per person

Hours: Monday–Thursday 11 a.m.–10 p.m., Friday–Saturday 11 a.m.–12 a.m., Sunday 12 p.m.–9 p.m.

Anna's Pizza No. 5
Food: Pizza, subs, veal/eggplant parmesan

115 Maury Ave.

(434) 977-6228

Cool Features: Family-owned and operated for 25 years. Take-out available.

Price: $5–$12 per person

Hours: Monday–Thursday 11 a.m.–10 p.m., Friday–Saturday 11 a.m.–11 p.m., Sunday 12 p.m.–10 p.m.

Arch's Frozen Yogurt

Food: Dessert foods (sandwiches and salads are now offered, too)

104 14th St. NW

(434) 984-2724

Cool Features: The best frozen yogurt ever!

Price: $4–$7 per person

Hours: Monday–Friday 9 a.m.–11 p.m., Saturday– Sunday 11 a.m.–11 p.m.

Awful Arthur's Seafood Company

Food: Seafood

333 W. Main St.

(434) 296-0969

Cool Features: Big-screen TV to watch games on, pool tables, darts.

Price: $13–$18 per person

Hours: Sunday–Thursday 11:30 a.m.–11 p.m., Friday– Saturday 11:30 a.m.–12 a.m., Bar 11:30 a.m.–2 a.m.

Baja Bean Company

Food: California Mexican

1327 W. Main St.

(434) 293-4507

Cool Features: Tuesday night karaoke!

Price: $6–$10 per person

Hours: Daily 11 a.m.–2 a.m.

Biltmore Grill

Food: American (burgers, sandwiches, a divine chocolate chip cookie pie desert)

16 Elliewood Ave.

(434) 293-6700

Cool Features: There's a big deck for outside seating, $2 drafts on Tuesday nights, on Thursdays from 8–9 p.m. every drink (no matter what it is) costs $1.

Price: $6–$13 per person

Hours: Daily 11 a.m.–10:30 p.m., Bar 11 a.m.–1:45 a.m.

Bizou

Food: American "upscale down-home cookin'" (seafood, steak, "smashed potatoes")

119 W. Main St., On the Downtown Mall

(434) 977-1818

Cool Features: This place has red booths and black- and-white movie posters everywhere!

Price: $7–$12

Hours: Monday–Thursday 11:30 a.m.–2:30 p.m., 5:30 p.m.–9 p.m., Friday–Saturday 11:30 a.m.–2:30 p.m., 5:30 p.m.–10 p.m.

Boar's Head Inn

Food: American, with a Southern touch

200 Ednam Dr.

(434) 296-2181

Price: $12–$25 per person

Hours: Monday–Saturday
11:30 a.m.–2 p.m.,
6 p.m.–9 p.m.

Bodo's Bagel Bakery

Food: Breakfast

Emmet St. and Preston Ave.

(434) 977-9598 (Emmet) and
(434) 293-5224 (Preston)

Cool Features: Everyone loves to go to Bodo's after a heavy night of drinking. It can sometimes seem very crowded on a Sunday morning, but the line moves right along.

Price: $3–$5 per person

Hours: Monday–Friday
6:30 a.m.–8 p.m.,
Saturday 7 a.m.–8 p.m.,
Sunday 8 a.m.–4 p.m.

Buddhist Biker Bar & Grill

Food: American (crab cakes, grilled BBQ shrimp, risotto cakes)

20 Elliewood Ave.

(434) 971-9181

Cool Features: Inside there is vaulted ceiling with a painted pond and suspended canoe

Price: $5–$20 per person

(Buddhist Biker, continued)

Hours: Monday–Saturday
5 p.m.–2 a.m.

C&O

Food: French/American (superb cheese plate and wine selection, three-course meals)

515 E. Water St.

(434) 971-7044

Cool Features: C&O is in one of the oldest buildings in Charlottesville, offering a quaint, historic atmosphere. A great place to take your parents for parent's weekend!

Price: $14–$26 per person

Hours: Sunday–Thursday
5:30 p.m.–10 p.m.,
Friday–Saturday
5:30 p.m.–11 p.m.

Coupe DeVille's

Food: American (sandwiches, Peruvian-style rotisserie)

9 Elliewood Ave.

(434) 977-3966

Cool Features: They have great live music outside on the terrace. *Rolling Stone* rated them very highly as having some of the best music in a college town.

Price: $7–$10 per person

Hours: Monday–Saturday
4 p.m.–2 a.m.

Duner's

Food: American (fresh seafood, meats, pasta, vegetarian options, fine desserts)

250 West in Ivy

(434) 293-8352

Price: $10–$19 per person

Hours: Daily 5 p.m.–10 p.m.

Escafe

Food: Asian/American with an international twist (cilantro and brie quesadillas, salads, vegetarian, soups)

Downtown Mall

(434) 295-8668

Cool Features: Great murals, lovely lighting, wonderful people-watching opportunities.

Price: $7–$10 per person

Hours: Tuesday–Wednesday 5:30 p.m.–12 a.m., Thursday–Saturday 5:30 p.m.–11 p.m., Sunday 4:30 p.m.–9:30 p.m.

Frank's Pizza

Food: Pizza, subs, pasta

109 14th St. NW

(434) 977-5700

Cool Features: Every Monday night they have a special deal—for $5.99 you can get a large cheese pizza and a 2-liter drink.

Price: $5 per person

Hours: Daily 11 a.m.–11 p.m.

Flaming Wok

Food: Chinese, Korean, Japanese

1305 Seminole Trail

(434) 974-6555

Cool Features: The chef prepares your meal right in front of you at your table—over flaming hot coals, no less!

Price: $7–$15 per person

Hours: Daily 11:30 a.m.–10 p.m.

Guadalajara

Food: Mexican

805 E. Market St., near the Downtown Mall

434-977-2676

Cool Features: Great Mexican food!

Price: $5–$7 per person

Hours: Daily 11 a.m.–10 p.m.

Hamilton's

Food: Contemporary gourmet American cuisine (fresh meats, game, crab cakes, vegetarian)

101 W. Main St., on the Downtown Mall

(434) 295-6649

Cool Features: Arty modern decor; lovely atmosphere. Hamilton's is very pricey—a good place to bring your parents for parents-weekend.

Price: $8–$21 per person

(Hamilton's, continued)

Hours: Lunch Monday–Saturday
11:30 a.m.–3 p.m.
Dinner Monday–Saturday
5:30 p.m.–10 p.m.

Hardware Store

Food: American (deli
sandwiches, salads, ribs,
crepes, seafood, burgers)

316 E. Main St., on the
Downtown Mall

(434) 977-1518

Cool Features: The Restaurant
space is 104 years old, and
a town landmark. There is a
bookshop directly below the
restaurant as well.

Price: $5–$20 per person

Hours: Monday–Thursday
11 a.m.–9 p.m.,
Friday–Saturday
11 a.m.–10 p.m.

Hotcakes

Food: Fancy, quick gourmet
meals pre-made (quiche, prime
rib, rosalita dip)

1137 Emmet St.,

(434) 295-6037

Cool Features: Nice
atmosphere, if you choose to
stay and eat in their little café.
Very good food.

Price: $5–$7 per person

Hours: Monday–Saturday
9 a.m.–8 p.m.

Jabberwocky

Food: American (new
expanded menu—all sorts
of sandwiches)

1517 University Ave.

(434) 984-4653

Cool Features: Always features
night entertainment (usually
with an okay band playing).

Price: $4–$9 per person

Hours: Daily 11 a.m.–2 a.m.

Liquid Vegetarian Cafè and Juice Bar

Food: Smoothies, vegetarian

109 Second St. SE

(434) 977-0117

Cool Features: Yummy
smoothies and all sorts of
vegetarian options!

Price: $4–$7 per person

Hours: Monday–Friday
8 a.m.–6 p.m., Saturday
9:30 a.m.–5 p.m.

Little John's

Food: Subs, salads,
muffins, brownies

1427 University Ave.,
on the Corner

(434) 977-0588

Cool Features: Students love to
come here for a late night bite.

Price: $5–$7 per person

Hours: Daily 24 hours

Martha's Café

Food: American (lots of vegetarian choices, pasta, salads, Asian theme)

11 Elliewood Ave.

(434) 971-7530

Cool Features: This restaurant is in a beautiful, old, blue house where students used to live in the '60s and '70s. The inside walls are covered with modern art. The bathroom has fish swimming in the bathtub.

Price: $5–$11 per person

Hours: Daily 11:30 a.m.–3 p.m., 5:30 p.m.–9 p.m.

Mellow Mushroom

Food: pizza, calzones, hoagies, and salads

1309 W. Main St.

(434) 972-9366

Cool Features: There's outside seating, lots of TVs, and strange inside decorations.

Price: Around $7 per person

Hours: Monday–Saturday 11 a.m.–2 a.m., Sunday 12 p.m.–2 a.m.

Michael's Bistro

Food: American (sandwiches, salads, fresh meats)

1427 University Ave., on the Corner

(434) 977-3697

(Michael's Bistro, continued)

Cool Features: There's a small balcony where you can sit at sunset and look out as far as the Blue Ridge. It also offers a great people-watcher's view of the Corner below.

Price: $4–$15 per person

Hours: Monday–Friday 11:30 a.m.–2:30 p.m., 5:30 p.m.–10 p.m., Bar open until 2 p.m. Saturday 12 p.m.–2:30 p.m., 3 p.m.–10 p.m., Bar open until 2 p.m.

Miller's

Food: American (steaks, seafood, sandwiches, vegetarian)

109 W. Main St., on the Downtown Mall

(434) 971-8511

Cool Features: Dave Matthews used to bartend here (supposedly it was his inspiration for the song entitled "Bartender" and many others). There is great live music here almost every night (Jazz night on Thursdays).

Price: $4–$18 per person

Hours: Monday–Saturday 10:30 a.m.–1:30 a.m., Sunday 12:30 p.m.–1:30 a.m.

Mono Loco

Food: Cuban

200 Water St.,
next to the Downtown Mall

(434) 979-0688

Cool Features: Beautiful décor, wonderful atmosphere. You can sit outside on a patio streamed with lights and lovely trees.

Price: $6–$16 per person

Hours: Monday–Friday
11:30 a.m.–2 p.m.,
5:30 p.m.–11:30 p.m.
Saturday 11:30 a.m.–2 p.m.,
5:30 p.m.–10:30 p.m.,
Sunday 11 a.m.–2 p.m.,
5:30 p.m.–10:30 p.m.

Moondance

Food: American (pasta, salmon, filet mignon)

201 E. Main St.,
on the Downtown Mall

(434) 984-3933

Cool Features: There's a front patio next to the Central Place Fountain in the middle of the Downtown Mall. Good people watching.

Price: $6–$20 per person

Hours: Monday–Saturday
11:30 a.m.–3 p.m.,
5:30 p.m.–10 p.m.

Northern Exposure

Food: American (pasta, pizza, steaks, sandwiches)

1202 W. Main St., just beyond the Corner going toward the Downtown Mall

(434) 977-6002

Cool Features: The restaurant is decorated in a NYC theme with subway maps and old black and white photographs.

Price: $5–$23 per person

Hours: Sunday–Thursday
11 a.m.–10 p.m., Friday–
Saturday 11 a.m.–11 p.m.

O'Neill's Irish Pub

Food: American/Irish (corned beef, fish & chips, burgers)

1505 University Ave.,
on the Corner

(434) 293-2029

Cool Features: On Thursdays, O'Neill's hosts the infamous Mug Night, where students bring in the biggest mug they can find and the bar will fill it to the brim with any beer on draft for only $2.

Price: $6–$9 per person

Hours: Every day 11 a.m.–
10 p.m., Bar open until 2 a.m.

Pita Pit

Food: Pita sandwiches with tons of toppings and different sauces

104 14th St. NW, just behind the Corner

(434) 977-PITA

Cool Features: You get to create your own pita!

Price: $4–$7 per person

Hours: Tuesday–Saturday 11:30 a.m.–3:30 a.m., Sunday–Monday 11:30 a.m.–1 a.m.

St. Marteen's Café

Food: American (hot wings, cheese fries)

1400 Wertland St., just behind the Corner

(434) 293-2233

Cool Features: The restaurant is filled with a Caribbean motif and a big UVA drinking scene.

Price: $5–$13 per person

Hours: Daily 11 a.m.–2 a.m. (late-night menu until 1 a.m.)

Southern Culture

Food: Cajun food (sweet potato fries, meatloaf, burgers, sandwiches, seafood)

633 W. Main St., between the Corner and the Downtown Mall

(434) 979-1990

Cool Features: The whole atmosphere is filled with a comfortable, old Southern feeling (sweeping curtains, creaking fans, pastel walls). There's also an outdoor patio.

Price: $6–$16 per person

Hours: Sunday 11 a.m.–2:30 p.m., Sunday–Thursday 5 p.m.–10 p.m., Friday–Saturday 5 p.m.–10:30 p.m.

Starr Hill Restaurant and Brewery

Food: American (crab cakes, award-winning brew master)

709 W. Main St., between the Corner and the Downtown Mall

(434) 977-0017

Cool Features: This is a great place to hear live music from touring bands. Supposedly, Faulkner's grandsons own this restaurant/bar.

Price: $12–$15 per person

Hours: Daily 4 p.m.–2 a.m.

Sticks

Food: American (meats on sticks, hummus, roasted eggplant, salads, rice)

917 Preston Ave.

(434) 295-5262

Cool Features: Offers a healthy alternative to fast food.

Price: $5–$7 per person

Hours: Monday–Saturday 11 a.m.–9 p.m.

Take it Away

Food: Deli sandwiches with great house dressings and fresh baked bread

115 Elliewood Ave., just off the Corner

(434) 295-1899

Cool Features: Very cool jazz music and beautiful posters and paintings to admire while you wait for a good sandwich. Students love to come here during the week in between classes and grab a lunch.

Price: $4–$7 per person

Hours: Monday–Saturday 10 a.m.–7 p.m.

Tavern

Food: Breakfast

Corner of Emmet St. and Barracks Rd.

(434) 295-0404

(Tavern, continued)

Cool Features: This breakfast spot is an old, historic fixture at UVA. On the roof is written in white letters, "Where Townspeople and Students Meet."

Price: $3–$6 per person

Hours: Daily 7 a.m.–3 p.m.

Thai '99

Food: Thai

2210 Fontaine Ave. Ext.

(434) 245-5263

Price: $7–$10 per person

Hours: Monday–Saturday 11 a.m.–2:30 p.m., 5 p.m.–9:30 p.m.

The Virginian

Food: American (great sandwiches—especially the BLT—crab cakes, steaks

1521 University Ave., on the Corner

434-984-4667

Cool Features: This is the oldest restaurant in Charlottesville. The walls are decorated with historic photographs of UVA boys who used to frequent here.

Price: $7–$11 per person

Hours: Sunday–Thursday 11 a.m.–10 p.m., Friday–Saturday 11 a.m.–11 p.m., Bar open until 2 a.m.

White Spot

Food: American (burgers, fries, gyros)

1407 University Ave., on the Corner

(434) 295-9899

Cool Features: This spot features the great "Gus Burger" (a fried egg on top of a burger), which has become a UVA late-night bite tradition at 2 a.m. after a wild night on the town.

Price: $5–$8 per person

Hours: Sunday–Tuesday 8 a.m.–11 p.m.

Did You Know?

The people of Charlottesville definitely know how to eat well. **There are many, many fabulous restaurants in town**—be sure to get to as many as you can. Also keep an eye out for some great food and wine festivals that frequently come to town throughout the year (such as the Vegetarian Festival, Taste of the Nation, and the Virginia Wine Festival).

Student Favorites:

Amigos Inc.
Baja Bean Company
Biltmore Grill
Bodo's Bagel Bakery
Café Europa
Little John's
Martha's Cafè
The Virginian
White Spot

Best Pizza:

Frank's Pizza

Best Chinese:

Flaming Wok

Best Breakfast:

Bodo's Bagel Bakery
Tavern

Best Wings:

Biltmore Grill

Best Healthy:

Café Europa
Martha's Cafè
Take it Away

Other Places to Check Out:

Christian's Pizza (East to West)
Daihachi (Sushi)
Rapture (International)
Vivace's (Italian)

Best Place to Take Your Parents:

Boar's Head Inn
C&O
Duner's
Southern Culture

Closest Grocery Stores:

Harris Teeter
975 Emmet St. N.
Barracks Shopping Center
(434) 984-2900

Kroger
1904 Emmet St. N
Barracks Shopping Center
(434) 295-8334

24-Hour Eating:

Little John's
Pita Pit
White Spot

Students Speak Out On...
Off-Campus Dining

"For food off grounds, Little John's is the favorite late-night place to find a greasy sub. During normal hours, I recommend Martha's Café, an off beat little place in a blue house on Elliewood Avenue."

"I think there is great food to be found in C-ville, contrary to popular belief—you just have to know where to find it. For sushi: Daihachi (off 29 near Outback Steakhouse), for Mexican: Guadalajara, not Baja Bean! For Cuban: Mono Loco—one of my favorites. East to West is probably my favorite, though. It's a little bit Asian, and a little bit American, and the 'celebs' of C-ville are known to go here, too. When I ate there, John Grisham was there celebrating his birthday. For pizza: Christian's Pizza or Frank's Pizza. For seafood: Awful Arthur's. For Southwestern: Southern Culture—this is definitely my favorite! It's not that well known to students, but it's absolutely the best food in town."

"There are great restaurants in Charlottesville, although most of them are on or around the Downtown Mall. On the Corner, there is Martha's Cafè off Elliewood Avenue (vegetarian options) and Little John's, which is notable just because it is open 24 hours, so a lot of people end up there really late coming from parties or the bars. There is a disgusting little diner that some will argue is a UVA tradition—the White Spot—but a hamburger with an egg on top has never appealed to me. Baja Bean is a great, convenient Mexican place, with huge portions and karaoke on Tuesday nights."

Q "**Great selection of restaurants off campus**. The Corner has something for everyone, and it's all quality (except maybe Baja Bean—I've always found them to be sub-par). There are a couple of nicer places on the Downtown Mall, too."

Q "The Corner has pretty good restaurants. The Downtown Mall has really nice places to eat. Students primarily go to the Corner because of its proximity, and the menu is more modest. I really like the Biltmore and St. Marteen's (get the cheese fries and try their hamburgers) – both on the Corner. After hours, **definitely hit up Little John's and Pita Pit**."

Q "Off campus, there is the Corner which has a ton of restaurants. There is really good food there! **All over Charlottesville, there are plenty of close places to eat**. You will never have a problem finding good food. Biltmore and Little John's are local favorites."

Q "There are some great places to eat around Charlottesville, from the delis to the nice restaurants. There are plenty of places to find good food. **There are more places to eat in Charlottesville than in most big cities**. You can try something new every week and not get bored."

Q "A few blocks away there is the Downtown Mall, which has excellent food and **all price ranges** (from cheap to expensive)."

Q "Off grounds there is a place called the Corner, right across the street from the Rotunda, with a number of excellent eateries and sandwich shops. **The best places are Little John's, Take It Away, Cafe Europa, Mellow Mushroom, and Frank's Pizza**."

Q "There are decent, cheap restaurants on the Corner that you can walk to. Off grounds, there are tons because we are right by 29, a major highway. Also, **downtown Charlottesville has a lot of nice café-type places**."

Q "We have so many restaurants off campus. I am going into my third year, and **there are still places I want to try**. We have downtown Charlottesville a couple miles away; a trolley takes you there for free."

Q "There is great food everywhere in Charlottesville. Just **ask, and you will find the good ones**."

Q "Good restaurants are on the Corner, on the Downtown Mall, and in other random places. On the Corner, **a good restaurant for American food is the Biltmore**, and for slightly more exciting food, there's Buddhist Biker Bar and Michael's Bistro. Another good place is Vivace's, and that has great Italian food and wine."

The College Prowler Take On...
Off-Campus Dining

Everyone agrees the restaurants in Charlottesville are fantastic and plentiful. The food quality and restaurant options in Charlottesville are what make it feel more like a big city. The Corner has tons of college-type cafés and restaurants that are fun and convenient. They offer pretty standard bar food for the most part (a hamburger and fries). For more varied food along the Corner, students enjoy Martha's, Take It Away, and Café Europa. The Downtown Mall has many amazing restaurants that feature even more adventurous food and wine (C&O, Rapture, Hamilton's, Escafe, and more). Of course, there are restaurants all over, but in Charlottesville there are definitely more really memorable and incredible places than not.

Don't be surprised if, by the time you graduate from UVA, there are restaurants in Charlottesville that you've never gotten a chance to sample. Generally, your first two years at UVA, you find yourself wrapped up more in the food on grounds and on the Corner, and sometimes you don't run into the hidden treasures that Charlottesville has to offer. In your later years, when transportation is easier and you are getting comfortable enough to be adventurous, you start to really see how much there is out there in Charlottesville dining. Try to get off-campus and out on the restaurant scene earlier in your college career; your stomach will thank you for it.

The College Prowler® Grade on

Off-Campus Dining: B+

A high Off-Campus Dining grade implies that off-campus restaurants are affordable, accessible, and worth visiting. Other factors include the variety of cuisine and the availability of alternative options (vegetarian, vegan, Kosher, etc.).

Campus Housing

The Lowdown On...
Campus Housing

Room Types:
Singles
Doubles

Best Dorms:
Old Dorms (McCormick Road Residence) when you're a first-year student.

After first year, live in Lambeth Dorms

Worst Dorms:
Hereford

Undergrads Living On Campus:
46%

Number of Dorms:
49

→

Dormitories:

Alderman Rd. Residence Area (13 dorms: Balz, Cauthen, Tuttle, Dunnington, Fitzhugh, Dunglison, Courtenay, Lile, Maupin, Webb, Watson, Dobie, and Woody Houses)

Floors: 3 floors each

Total Occupancy: Over 1600 total residents

Bathrooms: Three commodes and 2 showers (for each 10-person suite)

Coed: Yes, single sex by suite

Residents: All freshmen

Room Types: 5 doubles per suite (4 suites per floor)

Special Features: Outside, the suites on each floor are connected by one long balcony. There are also large meeting/study lounges, a computer lab, library, mailroom, Tuttle coffee house (in Tuttle), an ATM machine, and more. Each bedroom in Cauthen and Woody is furnished, including two beds and two wardrobes.

Bice House (9 apartments)

Floors: 7

Total Occupancy: 245

Bathrooms: Private (full-baths)

Coed: Yes

Residents: All upperclassmen

Room Types: Doubles and triples

Special Features: Each apartment has its own kitchenette with new cabinetry, sink, stove, and a refrigerator. A computer room is also provided for convenience, and there is a laundry room on the ground level.

Brown College at Monroe Hill (12 Dorms: Davis, Smith, Mallet, Long, Venable, Gildersleeve, McGuffey, Harrison, Tucker, Holmes, Rogers, and Peters Houses)

Floors: 3–4 floors each, all connected by underground tunnels

Total Occupancy: About 300 students each

Bathrooms: 2 commodes and 1 shower shared by 4 people in adjacent suites

Coed: Yes, alternating groups of suites

Residents: All freshmen

Room Types: Two single rooms in a suite

(Brown College at Monroe Hill, continued)

Special Features: Study lounge, kitchen, computer lab, TV lounges, library, laundry facilities, air-conditioning, fireplaces.

(Brown College requires a separate application in addition to the housing agreement form).

Copeley Apartments

Floors: 4 floors each

Total Ocupancy: 150 students

Bathrooms: Private (one full bath and one half bath per room)

Coed: Yes

Residents: All upperclasmen

Room Types: Apartments

Special Features: Each apartment has a full kitchen (does not include utensils, pots, pans, etc.), and a carpeted living room area.

Faulkner Apartments (Hench, Mitchell, and Younger)

Floors: 4 floors each

Total Ocupancy: 154 students

Bathrooms: Private (full baths)

Coed: Yes

Residents: All upperclasmen

Room Types: Apartments

(Faulkner Apartments, continued)

Special Features: There's a picnic area, laundry facilities, vending machines, and a computer room. All apartments are air conditioned and include free basic cable service in the living room.

Gooch/Dillard Residence Area

Floors: 4 floors each

Total Ocupancy: 655 students

Bathrooms: Private (2 baths)

Coed: Yes

Residents: All upperclasmen

Room Types: Six-person suites

Special Features: Beds, desks with study lamps, chairs, and Venetian blinds are provided. There are two kitchens located in buildings 382 and 388, and there are laundry facilities in buildings 382 and 387. The Runk Dining Hall is just a few steps away.

Hereford (5 houses: Johnson, Malone, Norris, Weedon, and Whyburn Houses)

Floors: Each house has 3 floors plus a basement

Total Occupancy: 500 students (100 of which are first years)

Bathrooms: 1 bathroom in each hall

(Hereford, continued)

Coed: Single sex by floor

Residents: Freshmen and upperclassmen

Room Types: Single and double rooms (All first-years live in doubles).

Special Features: The most diverse of all the dorms; air-conditioning, study lounges, computer lab, TV lounges, mailroom, dining hall, several laundry facilities.

Lambeth Residence Halls

Floors: 4 floors each

Total Occupancy: 840

Bathrooms: Suite

Coed: Yes, single sex by room

Residents: All upperclassmen

Room Types: Suites

Special Features: Laundry machines, vending machines, study lounges, and computer rooms are provided, and each suite has its own kitchen.

La Maison Française (The French House)

Floors: 3 floors

Total Occupancy: 35–40 students

Bathrooms: Private

Coed: Yes

Residents: All classes

(La Maison Française, continued)

Room Types: Mostly doubles and singles

Special Features: There are two washers and two dryers in the basement for residents' use. Every resident is assigned a box for receiving US mail, (messenger mail needs to be retrieved in the French department).

McCormick Road Residence (10 dorms: Page, Emmet, Kent, Dabney, Bonnycastle, Hancock, Metcalf, Lefevre, Humphreys, and Echols Houses)

Floors: 3-4 floors in each dorm

Total Occupancy: about 1300 students (125 in each dorm)

Bathrooms: Several community bathrooms on each floor

Coed: Single sex by floor

Residents: All freshmen

Room Types: All double rooms (with the exception of 30 small single rooms)

Special Features: Mailroom, "The Castle" snack bar (in Bonnycastle), vending machines, study lounges; McCormick is the most popular freshman housing option.

Munford/Gwathmey

Floors: 3 floors each

Total Occupancy: 125 in each dorm

Bathrooms: Ccommunity bathrooms on each floor

Coed: Yes

Residents: All classes

Room Types: Doubles and singles

Special Features: A number of kitchens and beautifully furnished lounges provide great space for residents to come together for formal programs or informal socializing.

Sprigg Lane (Lewis/Huxton)

Floors: 3 floors each

Total Occupancy: 100 in each dorm

Bathrooms: Private

Coed: Yes

Residents: All classes

Room Types: Mostly singles

Special Features: There is a study lounge with vending machines, and laundry facilities are provided. The rooms are furnished with beds, desks with chairs and bookshelves, and blinds or shades.

Bed Type

Single; twin extra-long

Cleaning Service?

Yes

What You Get

Air-conditioning (Hereford, Faulkner, and Brown only), bathrooms, computer labs, Ethernet connection, faculty advisors, (Brown and Hereford only), laundry facilities, mailroom, residential advisors, snack bars, study lounges, TV lounges, vending machines

Students Speak Out On...
Campus Housing

{ **"I lived in new dorms, but I wish I'd lived in the old dorms. The old dorms are a lot closer to classes. New dorms have some pros, though: suites and more diversity (old dorms are almost all white). Do not live in Hereford!"**

Q "New dorms are nicer but farther away. Typically, they don't create such a close-knit community with lots of people, just because you're in a suite with 10 people as opposed to the old dorms where you're in a hall with 30. **If you're a transfer student you should definitely try to get into Lambeth**—it's a bigger part of the party scene."

Q "**Do not live in Hereford, ever**. Old dorms are the place to live, meet people, and have fun, but the dorms are crap. But at least that way you have something to complain about together!"

Q "For first-year students, there seems to be a big split between new dorms and old dorms. New dorms have several rooms off of a common area and a shared bathroom, while old dorms have a hall-style arrangement. New dorms tend to be more diverse, **old dorms tend to be more social**. I lived in new dorms, but if I had to do it again, I might choose old dorms, just because I think there is greater potential for meeting people with the hall-style living."

Q "Try to **avoid dorms that are far away**. Dunglison and Courtney suck—you will spend so much time walking."

Q "For first year, live in old dorms. If you're going to live on grounds while an upperclassman, **definitely live in Lambeth**, because it's not too far from Grounds and it's right below Rugby Road (frat row)."

Q "**I think it's good to live on grounds your first two years** and then live in an apartment off grounds. It's a good taste of the real world—dealing with landlords and bills and all."

Q "There are new dorms and old dorms. New is suite-style, and old is hall-style. It just depends on which you prefer. I did suite-style, and I loved it, but **I have friends who choose old-style and loved it there**, too."

Q "**First-year dorms are okay**. I think the old dorms are the ones to stay away from; they are tiny."

Q "Hereford is not too good. **The new dorms are better**, but the old dorms are the best."

Q "They are your typical college dorms, and they're decent. I lived in the old dorms on McCormick Road and loved it. The new dorms are on Alderman; it's a great location, and it is really social. **Try not to get Hereford, because it's far away**, but I had friends everywhere, and they all loved where they were."

Q "Old dorms are definitely better. They aren't new or really nice, but they're great socially, and **the location is key**."

Q "**Dorms are very nice**. I would choose McCormick Road dorms—they are doubles, hallway-style. Alderman is suite-style with five doubles all attached to a large common room. They are all good, but I like McCormick Road best because that's where I lived."

Q "Live in the old dorms on McCormick Road. They have cooler people, and it is much closer! **If you get new ones on Alderman, it isn't the end of the world**. I lived in old, so I am biased."

Q "Just don't live in Hereford or Gooch/Dillard, because those are really far away. **I think sometimes people get moved there as a punishment**."

Q "All of the dorms are pretty nice, but if you stay on campus, **do not get a single room because they are too small to live in**."

The College Prowler Take On...
Campus Housing

Most all students agree that the old dorms (McCormick Road Resident Area) are the place to be your first year. Despite the small double rooms, they are far more social, and the location is much more convenient for classes and other activities. The only place to especially avoid is Hereford—this seems to be a consensus across campus. These dorms are much farther away from almost everything, and you will spend much of your time as a first-year student feeling very isolated. Many students, no matter where they live, are happy with campus housing. A lot of it depends on who you live with, rather than where you live—some people luck out with an awesome roommate, while others aren't so fortunate. Generally, though, people in old dorms are more satisfied with their first-year living experience than people in other locations. If by chance you get stuck in an undesirable dorm, there's really nothing to fear. Simply make the best of it: go in with a good attitude, be friendly and open, and chances are you'll end up loving where you are. UVA is so big that odds are you'll find someone you enjoy hanging out with.

In terms of quality, the dorm facilities at UVA are pretty standard. Because there are definitely those dorms that many don't want to live in, and because the housing office is not very courteous (especially to those students who must move back on grounds after being off grounds), it's best to get out of campus housing after a year or two. For incoming students, whether they be transfers or first-years, and those who aren't ready for their own apartments yet, UVA's dorms are more than adequate.

B-

The College Prowler® Grade on
Campus Housing: B-

A high Campus Housing grade indicates that dorms are clean, well-maintained, and spacious. Other determining factors include variety of dorms, proximity to classes, and social atmosphere.

Off-Campus Housing

The Lowdown On...
Off-Campus Housing

Undergrads in Off-Campus Housing:
53%

Average Rent For:
Studio Apt.: $615 per month
1BR Apt.: $740 per month
2BR Apt.: $950 per month

Best Time to Look for a Place:
Early fall (September/October)

Popular Areas:
14th Street
Rugby Road

For Assistance Contact:
www.universityoffgrounds.com

Management Services Corporation (MSC)

PO Box 5306,
Charlottesville, VA 22905

(434) 977-8203

www.msc-rents.com

msc@msc-rents.com

CBS

PO Box 3344,
Charlottesville, VA 22903

(434) 971-9922

www.cbsrentals.com

cbsrentals@rlc.net

Shamrock Corporation

PO Box 3932,
Charlottesville, VA 22903

(434) 979-7307

ShamrockCorp@aol.com

Veliky Reality

PO Box 6711,
Charlottesville, VA 22906

(434) 293-5358

www.velikyrentals.com

office@velikyrentals.com

Did You Know?

Most students decide to move off Grounds after first year. It has become a sort of tradition. Even in the early fall when students first get to UVA, many start looking around for both people they might want to live with and for where they might want to be. Of course, try not to get stressed out by what a lot of people may be doing. Lease signing starts in October, but there are almost always places still left even as late as the August before classes start. **Don't be too hasty with decisions**; remember that you are choosing very important things for all of your second year—your home and your roommates.

Students Speak Out On...
Off-Campus Housing

> "Off-campus housing is definitely worth it. Live off Grounds ASAP! I recommend JPA or the 14th Street area. I've lived in different sections throughout my stay here, and those are the best options."

Q "I lived in a fraternity house for the three years after my first year. It was great. If you are interested in a fraternity, don't go signing a lease for some place a couple of months into your first year, as **you may want to think about living in the house**."

Q "In my experience, about half of students move off Grounds after their first year. I think it all depends on the location of your apartment and how responsible your management company is. **My roommates and I had good experiences with MSC**, which owns many apartments in the area."

Q "I think it's definitely worth it. Obviously, the closer it is to grounds, the more you're going to pay. That's also the case if you choose to live by yourself. Always be on top of your rental agency, **make sure you know what you're signing up for**."

Q "**It's definitely worth it!**"

Q "**It's too expensive for me**. It's hard to find something close to grounds, decent, and not too expensive."

Q "**Most of the off-grounds housing are actually closer to grounds** than on-grounds housing."

Q "It's definitely worth it to live off grounds. **It's kind of hard to throw a party on grounds**."

Q "Starting after first semester, **begin looking for housing for second year so you'll have first pick**. Otherwise, it gets limited, shady, and pricey."

Q "You can get a three-bedroom place for $900 a month if you're lucky, but **there are a lot of overpriced places**."

Q "It is much cheaper to live on grounds than off grounds, because you are closer in terms of proximity to your classes and the various facilities. **When you're on grounds, you can have Virginia busing**."

Q "I'm going to be a second-year student, so I've only lived on campus, but next year I'll have an apartment. You have to get a place early, but **there are tons of places, and buses run everywhere**. Most people move off after their first year."

Q "It's very convenient here. You won't have a problem getting a house or apartment at all; although, **some of it is expensive**."

Q "**There is a ton of off-campus housing**, and most people move off when they get older. It is really nice. The apartments are really good, but the houses are kind of old."

Q "I did it for three years. **You got to sign leases in October, which is the only bummer**. Besides that, everything is in a five-block radius from campus."

Q "It's kind of weird getting a lease signed because you have to decide really early, and you don't always know the people that you will live with that well. **It's a process, but it all works out**."

Q "A lot of off-campus housing is literally steps away from campus. If you want to live off campus, it makes school a lot cheaper. **If you have a car, it definitely doesn't cause any inconvenience**."

The College Prowler Take On...
Off-Campus Housing

Most students think living off grounds is definitely worth it. Not only do you get a taste of the real world, but in doing so, you generally have an absolute blast. There are drawbacks in having to decide so early on (fall/winter of first year) whether or not to sign a lease and with whom you will live the following year. Certainly, there is a lot of pressure, and at first, it is a bit overwhelming setting up and paying the monthly rent and utilities, but the payoff is great. Students generally love the freedom, the fun, and the comfortable feel of living in your own place surrounded by virtually all students in their own houses or apartments—not to mention that the house/apartment parties are great.

In terms of convenience, many students are ambivalent. Location tends to determine price, so it largely depends on what you're willing to pay. Some find it less costly and easier to continue living on grounds; others find off grounds is just as convenient, especially if it is located near a bus stop, within walking distance, or if someone in the house has a car. A large percentage of Virginia's students end up living off campus sometime during their college career, and Charlottesville is a good town for student-friendly housing, as long as you're willing to look for good deals and commit early.

The College Prowler® Grade on
Off-Campus
Housing: A-

A high grade in Off-Campus Housing indicates that apartments are of high quality, close to campus, affordable, and easy to secure.

Diversity

The Lowdown On...
Diversity

Native American:
Less than 1%

White:
73%

Asian American:
11%

International:
5%

African American:
9%

Out-of-State:
28%

Hispanic:
2%

Political Activity

Charlottesville, while being a wonderful place to spend your four-year college experience, can be too sheltered from what's going on in the world. Obviously some events (like the war in Iraq) bring out a lot of passion in the student population, and there are plenty of active organizations that feed this political passion among those students (Critical Mass, Take Back the Night, Amnesty International, Children of War, European Society, The Declaration, and Republican and Democrat Organizations). Overall, however, the UVA student body can seem somewhat apathetic and insulated from political matters.

Gay Pride

UVA is becoming increasingly more accepting of its gay and lesbian population. There are various active organizations at the University promoting gay awareness (Gay and Lesbian Christian Students Association, the Missionary, Out on Rugby, and the Queer Student Union). It took a while for UVA to get to this stage, though, and there is still evidence of intolerance in many places.

Most Popular Religions

There are a few prominent Christian groups within the University that regularly hold meetings. Some religious groups include: the Baptist Student Union, Buddhist Meditation Society, Campus Crusade for Christ, Chabad Jewish Heritage Student Association, Korean Catholic Student Ministry, Muslim Students Association, Quaker Worship Group, and many more. However, keeping true to Jefferson's ideal of the separation of church and state, there is no one religious affiliation associated with the University. In fact, the school chapel is noticeably isolated from the rest of the grounds.

Economic Status

UVA students come off as pretty wealthy—with their cars, clothes, and drinking habits, it would seem they would have to be. However, there are plenty of students on financial aid, student loans, and scholarships. While many are from the upper/middle-class, there is a bit of diversity in economic backgrounds.

Minority Clubs

There are many minority clubs at UVA, including the Black Student Union, Afghan Student Organization, Arab Student Organization, Asian Student Union, Black Student Alliance, Graduate Women in Business, Latin American Students Association, National Organization for Women at UVA, Society of the Virginia Irish, Society of Women Engineers, Society for the Promotion of Indian Classical Music and Culture Among Youth (SPIC-MACAY), Zeta Phi Beta Sorority, and the Lesbian, Gay, Bisexual, Transgender Union. Some of these groups have a much bigger presence on grounds than others—e.g., the Black Student Union and the National Organization for Women at UVA.

Students Speak Out On...
Diversity

{ **"It is pretty diverse. First year, I had maybe two American friends, but that had a lot to do with where I was living (Hereford)."**

"There's a lot of **self-segregation**."

"UVA has its share of ethnic diversity; however, blending to achieve a functional diversity seems more of a challenge. The African American students have been accused of self-segregation, which I found during my time at UVA to be a huge social force. Of course, there is likely self-segregation on the parts of the **white students from Northern Virginia**, as well."

"Diversity on campus sucks. There are diverse ethnicities, but they don't intermingle so much. **African Americans tend to stick together** and the Black Student Alliance has this philosophy about bonding within their own little community and helping each other out. I'm sure they would readily disagree with me, but it is true that black-white relations at UVA suck."

"**I think it's more diverse than it should be**. I think in recent years the acceptance process might have become a little flawed, and not based entirely on qualifications."

"I like that UVA has a diverse crowd, but because UVA is so diverse, **there are some tensions that come to the surface sometimes**."

Q "The campus is very diverse. **There are more minorities going to Virginia now than ever**."

Q "There's a lot of diversity and clubs and stuff, but there's also some self-segregation. We're trying to work on that. Like, my sorority is maybe going to try to have a party with one of the fraternities from the black fraternal council. I know it sounds normal, but **at Virginia it's kind of a new concept**. I'm excited—that would be fun."

Q "It's pretty diverse, but like most places, people segregate themselves. **I am not the standard WASP**, and I've had no problems at all here."

Q "It's somewhat diverse, but honestly, **people stick to their cultures more than I would like**."

Q "Racially, and probably socio-economically, it really isn't too diverse. But **if you look at people individually, everyone is so interesting**, intelligent, fascinating, and diverse as human beings."

Q "**Virginia's diversity is great**, and it's growing everyday."

Q "It's very diverse. **It's nice, but everyone sticks to their own cliques**; so, if you try to meet people, it is diverse, but if you don't, it's not."

Q "You get a mix on campus, but **mostly the students are white and from the South**."

The College Prowler Take On...
Diversity

Student opinion varies a great deal on diversity issues. Some believe that diversity at UVA is good and getting better, while others see the University as primarily a rich-white-kid school. Much of this depends on personal experience. Many students have encountered self-segregation among the various campus groups, and feel this is one of the biggest barriers to a functioning diversity. The best way to experience diversity at Virginia is to seek it out for yourself—there are many different people at the school, once you get past social cliques.

Overall, UVA could do better with diversity, but at least the administration recognizes this, and is trying to promote a new look for the school. Tolerance and political involvement are getting better, and despite the self-segregation, there are still days when you'll be surprised at how many languages you hear spoken, or the mix of different students you see studying together in the library.

C

The College Prowler® Grade on
Diversity: C

A high grade in Diversity indicates that ethnic minorities and international students have a notable presence on campus and that students of different economic backgrounds, religious beliefs, and sexual preferences are well-represented.

Guys & Girls

The Lowdown On...
Guys & Girls

Men Undergrads:
47%

Women Undergrads:
53%

Birth Control Available?

Yes. The pill, the patch, the ring, the shot—basically everything is offered. Call (434) 924-2773 a few weeks in advance to schedule an appointment. Sometimes, they get really backed up, so the earlier you call the better. It is also helpful and less intimidating to talk with a PHE (Peer Health Educator) about these sorts of things, in addition to a gynecologist. The Peer Health Educator is usually an upperclassman who is fully trained and has all sorts of important information about both men's and women's health.

Social Scene

The UVA social scene is difficult to define. Certainly, Greek life makes up a lot of it, though definitely not as much as it used to. But while the school holds tight to many of its traditions—Greek life included—UVA is expanding to include a variety of different social scenes as more and more different people join the community. Students are generally outgoing, friendly, and interested in what they do; the social scene is a huge part of student life.

Hookups or Relationships?

UVA can be odd and sometimes frustrating in terms of relationships, dating, and hookups. Often, you'll find two types of people: those who randomly hook up at frat parties and bars, and those who are in extremely serious relationships that will probably culminate in marriage after graduation. There is very little casual dating that comes in between.

Best Place to Meet Guys/Girls

Typically, classes, student organizations, sport's teams, mutual friends, and parties are all great ways to meet new people.

Dress Code

UVA's social dress code is quite distinct and easily followed, if you have the desire to strut your stuff:

Guys – Polo shirt with the collar flipped up, khakis or jeans, flip-flops or reefs, orange visor or baseball hats, and sometimes the fratty pants (all plaid, sort of ridiculous looking).

Girls – Tiny skirts or capri pants, button-down pink blouses or extra-tight tank-tops, pearls, flip-flops, lots of makeup.

Did You Know?

Top Places to Find Hotties:

1. Classes
2. Bars
3. Frats

Top Places to Hook Up:

1. Frats
2. Any party
3. Football games
4. Dorms/houses/apartments
5. The lawn

Students Speak Out On...
Guys & Girls

> "That first day of spring when all the girls jump into skimpy summer clothing for the first time and start sunbathing on the Lawn and the Quad is a great day. There are a bunch of attractive people at UVA."

Q "While there is a mix of all types of students at UVA, in my experience there are two dominant subtypes. The guy: dressed in khakis, flip-flops even in the winter, polo shirt with the collar turned up making him look something like a confused magician, and bag slung over his shoulder. The girl: spent hours on her hair this morning to impress the polo boy, carrying the latest Kate Spade bag over one shoulder (no matter how heavy her books are), wearing a tank top and skirt even as it becomes too cold to be comfortable, and either Reef flip-flops or a high-heel version. Both guys and girls seem ridiculous. I suppose **we have a reputation for being good-looking**, but I think that comes with a healthy dose of snottiness."

Q "**Everyone here is pretty attractive, guys and girls**. There are virtually no fat people. Everyone runs and works out at the gyms. The gyms are really great, by the way!"

Q "Most UVA people are very attractive. The girls are qualitatively and quantitatively good-looking. It's all the same type of good looking among the guys—**there's not a lot of variety among the pink polos, khaki shorts**, and orange Abercrombie visors"

Q "**There're a lot of hot guys, and they know it**, which defeats the purpose of them being hot. There are a lot of girls I can't stand here, too."

Q "The girls are way hotter than the guys. **It's good for me, since I'm a guy**."

Q "There are lots of good-looking people on campus. **Virginia has a reputation for having hot guys**, so that's such a bonus. The girls here are mixed, but there are plenty of guys to choose from."

Q "**Everyone is laid-back** and willing to help you out or become friends with you."

Q "In general, most are hot… but not everyone, though. **In general, they are preppy**."

Q "Every guy has a short haircut, hemp necklace, khakis, hat, and sandals—it's amazing. Girls are all about makeup and dressing up**. The girls might be attractive if they would get rid of the perfume and makeup**. The guys, too; they need to not be dumb frat boys."

Q "The guys are, for the most part, pretty preppy. A lot are very Southern; it's a mix of hot and not. There are lots of pretty girls. **I think everyone at Virginia works out**."

Q "Guys and girls are both really nice. **I find the Southern culture to be really genteel**, on the whole. The boys are really cute, in a frat-guy sort of way. I really love how they dress."

Q "My guy friends tell me that the girls are really nice down here. I agree. **The men, if I must speak for them, are also quite the catch**! The people are attractive!"

Q "Girls are nice and guys are, too. **There is a little rift between the 'rich Southerners' and the normal people**, but this is not a problem and not really much of a rift. Depending upon what you're like, you may find yourself laughing at some of the outfits sometimes—people get all dressed up, but I like it. It makes us unique."

Q "The chicks are pretty good. **I have been told that the guys are better**, but my friends found crazy hot girls whenever they wanted."

Q "The guys are mostly shaggy-haired preppy boys, but if you like more northern boys, there are some of them, too. The girls are pretty much the same, just pretty preppy. Everyone is preppy, smart, and mostly in shape. Most of the people at the school are very attractive. **It's like a little utopia**."

Q "**There are some really hot girls here**. If you are looking for guys, there are a lot of us, too."

Q "When you get here, **people will not be as mature**. About two-thirds of the school is from Northern VA, so they will all know each other, since they come from the same high school."

Q "I'm from Brooklyn, so there was a big culture shock for me when I came down to UVA. Girls here love guys from New York, which is a plus, and the chicks here are definitely really hot, although not as diverse as the girls back home. **I love the fact that the girls here get all dressed up for class**!"

The College Prowler Take On...
Guys & Girls

UVA students have a very refined look. Most really care about appearances, so you will certainly see a lot of dressing up for class, as well as a lot of running around grounds and working out at the gym. Some find this to be a cute and distinctive feature of UVA, while others find it obnoxious and superficial. Most students agree the girls are way hotter than the guys. Personality-wise, however, there is some definite snobbiness that's found more within the girl population and detracts from better looks. The guys are mainly fratty—many complete with shaggy hair, an Abercrombie suit, and a beer gut.

It is remarkable how similar people look at UVA, in their clothes and actions. While this probably isn't true when you get down to the deeper levels, superficially there is a lot of the same thing. This can either be boring and unfortunate, or reliable and comforting, depending on how you look at it. In general, people are very friendly and outgoing, with a wonderful laid-back sense of humor; there is certainly a degree of snobbiness, but you can get past this without too much trouble. The more you become involved in different activities and organizations, the more you'll become exposed to different sorts of people—not just the ones who define UVA's style from afar.

The College Prowler® Grade on
Guys: B+

A high grade for Guys indicates that the male population on campus is attractive, smart, friendly, and engaging, and that the school has a decent ratio of guys to girls.

The College Prowler® Grade on
Girls: A-

A high grade for Girls not only implies that the women on campus are attractive, smart, friendly, and engaging, but also that there is a fair ratio of girls to guys.

Athletics

The Lowdown On...
Athletics

Athletic Division:
NCAA Division I

Conference:
Atlantic Coast Conference
(ACC)

School Mascot:
The Cavalier

**Males Playing
Varsity Sports:**
368 (6%)

**Females Playing
Varsity Sports:**
290 (4%)

Men's Varsity Sports:

Baseball

Basketball

Cross-Country

Football

Golf

Lacrosse

Soccer

Swimming & Diving

Tennis

Track & Field

Wrestling

Women's Varsity Sports:

Basketball

Cross-Country

Field Hockey

Golf

Lacrosse

Rowing

Soccer

Softball

Swimming & Diving

Tennis

Track & Field

Volleyball

Club Sports:

Archery

Badminton

Belly Dance Club

Ballroom Dance

Brazilian Jiu-Jitsu

Capoeira

Cavalier Road Runners

Cricket

Cycling

Diving

Etcetera Winterguard

Fencing

Field Hockey

ISKF Karate

Judo

Mahogany Dance Troupe

Myo Sim Karate

Rhapsody Dance Ensemble

Rugby

Sailing

Shotokan Karate

Soccer

Squash

Tae Kwon Do

Tennis

Ultimate Frisbee

University Dance Club

Virginia Alpine Ski Team

Virginia Dance Company

Virginia Golf Club

(Club Sports, continued)
Virginia Swim Club
Virginia Rowing Association
Virginia Soccer League
Volleyball
Water Polo

Intramurals:
Basketball
Flag Football
Field Hockey
Inner Tube Water Polo
Soccer
Softball
Tennis
Volleyball

Getting Tickets

Students can get into any athletic event for free with their student ID. Everyone else must purchase tickets for the following sports during regular season: football, basketball (men's and women's), baseball, soccer (men's and women's), and lacrosse (men's and women's). There is also an admission charge for any ACC or NCAA championship events.

The Virginia Athletic Ticket Office is located in Bryant Hall at the Carl Smith Center (off Stadium Road).

Virginia Athletic Ticket Office
PO Box 400826
Charlottesville, VA 22904-4826

Office Hours: Monday–Friday 9 a.m.–5 p.m.

(800) 542-UVA1 or (434) 924-UVA1

Fax: (434) 243-3571

Most Popular Sports

Football, basketball, soccer, lacrosse (in that order)

Best Place to Take a Walk

Around the grounds (particularly on or through the lawn)

Gyms/Facilities

Aquatic and Fitness Center (AFC)

Dell Basketball Courts

Memorial Gym

North Grounds Recreation Center

Outdoor Recreation Center

Perry-Fishburne Tennis Courts

Slaughter Recreation Center

Snyder Tennis Center

Students Speak Out On...
Athletics

"Basketball is big here—some of the crazier fans (like me) have been known to camp out for weeks in the snow and rain just to get the closest seats to the floor. It's ACC basketball, need I say more?"

Q "Things are big for different people. Varsity football is huge, and soccer and lacrosse have decent followings, as well. IM sports are a great time, but they require some initiative—as in you have to go sign up for them. **Usually dorms or fraternities or other organizations put together little teams** to compete in flag football, Frisbee, soccer, and more. Pretty fun."

Q "I don't think IM sports are that big at all—I never really heard about them. **Obviously basketball and football are huge**. It is a big tradition to go to the football games, but it's not for everyone."

Q "**Varsity football and basketball** are pretty big."

Q "Sports are huge! UVA has a couple dozen varsity teams that are extremely competitive. You don't become a UVA student until you go to a UVA football and basketball game, but **if you'd rather participate instead of spectate, intramurals have a lot to offer**."

Q "**Both varsity sports and IM sports are very big**. I would recommend IM sports to anyone who attends."

Q "IM sports are always available, and I guess they're pretty big. Varsity basketball is a pretty big deal. We beat Duke two years in a row, so I guess that was a big deal. We're not that great, but I'd say we're better than average. Our football team is also a big deal, but it's not really all that great. **Everyone gets dressed up for football games, and we sing a song every time we have a touchdown**. The school is full of tradition."

Q "IMs are great. I played football, basketball, soccer, softball, and floor hockey. Virginia football dominates weekends. There are pre-games everywhere, at the Lawn, at frats, or at people's apartments. **Virginia basketball is nuts; people camp out for weeks to go to the games**."

Q "**Tons of people participate in IMs**. There are dorm leagues, frat leagues, coed leagues, independent leagues—tons of leagues and tons of IMs. Varsity sports are also big, especially football and basketball."

Q "Both intramurals and varsity sports are pretty big. **Football and basketball games are huge events** and lots of fun."

Q "**I'm not much into sports**, but basketball games are fun to attend. Our football team has been sucking, and so has our basketball, but they are still fun to go to."

Q "If you want to play IM sports, you will be able to. There are also clubs sports, as well. **You can try to walk onto a team at Virginia**, but you better be good."

Q "**The football games are awesome, and everyone goes**! The basketball and soccer games get just as many students out there, too. There are always a ton of parties afterwards."

The College Prowler Take On...
Athletics

Athletics at UVA have always been huge, and most everyone recognizes this coming into the school. Basketball and football in particular are very big sports here, no matter the quality of the team from season to season. Going to home football games is definitely a tradition at UVA; students get all dressed up, go to tailgates beforehand, and sing the "Good 'Ole Song" after every touchdown. In many ways, it's true that you don't get the full experience at Virginia until you've been to a sporting event. Certainly, there are students who hate going to the games and just don't; however, it is a good thing to go to at least one and see what it's all about before you write it off completely. Intramurals and club sports also have a pretty big presence on grounds. Almost any sport you can think of is offered. UVA students enjoy watching sports and being active.

Some say the reason UVA has a tradition of dressing up for games is that, years ago, the teams were so bad that students felt that if the teams couldn't look good, at least the fans would. This tradition sums up the good humor and fun nature of Virginia spectators. Many refuse to participate, and this is perfectly all right, but it can be fun to dress up for a few games. There is plenty to find in Virginia's athletics, at all levels of competition.

The College Prowler® Grade on

Athletics: A

A high grade in Athletics indicates that students have school spirit, that sports programs are respected, that games are well-attended, and that intramurals are a prominent part of student life.

Nightlife

The Lowdown On...
Nightlife

Club and Bar Prowler: Popular Nightlife Spots!

Unfortunately, there is hardly a club scene in Charlottesville. The only "real" club is Club 216 along the Downtown Mall.

Club 216

218 W. Water St., Ste. F
(434) 296-8783
www.club216.com
Hours: Friday–Saturday
10 p.m.–5 a.m.

(Club 216, continued)

This is Charlottesville's only gay and lesbian bar/dance club (and its only club, period). It is really very fun, but unfortunately, you need to be a member or know a member to get in. Occasionally, there will be open Saturdays where anyone can get in for $12.

Escafe

Downtown Mall (under Eastern Standard Restaurant)
(434) 295-8668

This is a great little restaurant/café (see the off-campus dining section)—very hip and

➜

(Escafe, continued)

trendy. Late night, it turns into somewhat of a club scene. There are raves, discos, and dancing Thursdays and some weekends. Door admission.

Star Hill Restaurant & Brewery

709 Main St. W

(434) 977-0017

This is more of a live-music club than a dancing club, located right across from the train station, between the Corner and the Downtown Mall. Supposedly owned by William Faulkner's grandsons, Star Hill has somewhat replaced an old town favorite, Traxx, where the likes of incredible musicians (Tim Reynolds, Dave Matthews, and Elliot Smith) used to play. Norah Jones and Dispatch, among many other talented artists, have played here in the last year. Buy tickets in advance or at the door.

Bar Prowler:

Most students go up to the Corner to one of the restaurant-by-day, bar-by-night spots, simply because the Corner is within walking distance to most student housing and has a very casual, laid-back feel to it.

(Bar Prowler, continued)

The Downtown Mall, however, has a pretty classy, more "grown-up" bar scene that students generally don't get into as much.

Jabberwocky

1517 University Ave., along the Corner

(434) 984-4653

Recently re-modeled and re-named, this old favorite now features a lot of live music all week long. Very dark, very smokey, very loud, and mostly very crowded, this atmosphere can sometimes get too stifling. Generally, this scene adopts a particular, loyal following among students.

Michael's Bistro

1427 University Ave., along the Corner

(434) 977-3697

www.skylinemall.com/bistro/

One of the few great-quality restaurants along the Corner, Michael's Bistro is also a fun bar that features some good live music, ranging from jazz, blues, funk, and folk. Most shows are free.

Miller's

109 W. Main Street,
on the Downtown Mall

(434) 971-8511

www.millersdowntown.com

This is an old Charlottesville fixture, a well-known blues and jazz venue. Famous for a little-known struggling artist named Dave Matthews who used to bartend there to make rent. A very popular, laid-back bar that is almost always crowded and smokey. Thursday nights are jazz nights, featuring the area's brilliant jazz musicians like John D'Earth and company. There is door admission of $3–$5.

O'Neill's Irish Pub

1505 University Ave.,
on the Corner

Charlottesville, VA 22903

(434) 293-2029

O'Neill's is another student favorite Corner bar/restaurant. Equipped with pool tables, two full bars (one upstairs and downstairs), and a jukebox, O'Neill's is packed mostly on Thursday nights for Mug Night. Students bring in the biggest mug, glass, or container they can find, and bartenders fill it to the brim every time for only $2.

St. Marteen's Café

1400 Wertland St.,
behind the Corner

(434) 293-2233

Students who want to just sit around in a booth, eat cheese fries late at night, and drink exotic (often dirty-sounding) drinks that they've never heard of before love to come to St. Marteen's.

Tokyo Rose

13 University Shopping Center, in the Ivy Road Shopping Center

(434) 296-3366

It's a cool sushi bar by day, and a fun music and dance club by night. The music featured is new and up-and-coming indie rock. There are acoustic performances on Tuesday nights upstairs.

The Virginian

1521 University Ave.,
along the Corner

Charlottesville, VA 22903

(434) 984-4667

An old fixture of the UVA/Charlottesville community—though very cramped and noisy, students still love to come here. There's a drink special almost every night.

Bars Close At:

2 a.m.

Primary Areas with Nightlife:

The Corner

The Downtown Mall

Cheapest Place to Get a Drink:

Biltmore and O'Neill's on Thursday nights; Amigos on Wednesday nights

Favorite Drinking Games:

Beer Pong

Card Games

Never Have I Ever

Power Hour

Student Favorites
(See Off-Campus Dining):

Amigos Inc.

Baja Bean

Biltmore Grille

Club 216

Coupe Deville's

Frat Parties

Jabberwocky

Miller's

O'Neill's Irish Pub

Star Hill Restaurant & Brewery

The Virginian

Useful Resources for Nightlife:

www.dailyprogress.com

www.virginiamusicflash.com/ vmf/charlottclubs.htm

The Hook Magazine

What to Do if You're Not 21

Even if you're not 21, it is very easy to get a hold of some alcohol—either at frat parties or organization parties. Sometimes, there is even a bit of drinking in the dorms, though this is strictly prohibited. Of course, there are plenty of other things to do, as well: movies, ice-skating, bowling, concerts, eating, and hanging out with friends. Also check out:

Prism Coffeehouse

214 Rugby Rd.

Charlottesville, VA 22903

(434) 977-7476

Features folk, bluegrass, and international acts and music on tour. Eccentric, cozy, old, white house stuck in the middle of frat row. It's closed during the summer months.

Organization Parties

There are plenty of organization parties at UVA, especially since Virginia students are so big on being involved and active with the organizations that they care about. Some of the organizations are particularly known for their parties: First Year Players (FYP), University Guides, any a cappella groups' parties, and the Cavalier Daily. These parties are open to members of the organization and usually friends of members. Fraternities and sororities also have date functions, semi-formals, and formals besides their regular parties that are generally a blast, considering how much money is put into them.

Frats

See the Greek section!

Students Speak Out On...
Nightlife

"Ugh, the nightlife is not good. The frat scene is huge and very sucky. There are no clubs (okay, except 216—which is not very popular with straight guys). The good bars are on the Corner or the Downtown Mall."

Q "I personally think that frat parties are dirty with crappy beer. The majority of bars on the Corner (O'Neill's and Jabberwocky) are the same way, except you pay for the crappy beer. It's not to say it isn't fun, **it just gets tiring after a while**."

Q "There's one dance club called 216, but I've never been. Most good parties on campus (and off) in the area take place at the fraternities. Some are very, very cool; others are very, very not. You just have to look around. Usually, fraternities develop regular crowds as certain people decide where they like to party. Also, **just about any organization you join will have parties at some point**. Bars are fun, but make sure your ID is good. I recommend Buddhist Biker Bar, Coupe Deville's, and the Biltmore. Other bars on the Downtown Mall are fun, too. (Rapture is one.) Transportation can be a problem, however."

Q "**The nightlife is okay the first couple of years**. Frat parties are the thing to do the first two years, because that's how you meet a lot of people, but you grow out of it."

Q "Clubs? What clubs? Unless you're gay and want to buy a membership to Club 216, there aren't any. Most of the **parties that students go to are frat parties**—they always involve alcohol."

Q "Definitely hit up a frat party first or second year because the beer's free, and there's a lot of hot people there. Once you have an ID, legal or not, definitely go to the bars on the Corner. **Go to a bar if you don't want to bump and grind** and want more meaningful conversation. Jabberwocky has some pretty good drink specials and happy hours. If you want to hear really good live music, definitely go to Coupe's Wednesday nights. There's margarita nights at Amigos, and karaoke Tuesday nights at Baja Bean."

Q "I don't know if you read Rolling Stone, but **Coupe Deville's was rated very highly** as one of the top college bars, and it's on the Corner—the place that's right off grounds and has lots of shops and restaurants. Biltmore, Buddhist, and O'Neill's Irish Pub are some other good places, too."

Q "There are no clubs unless you drive to DC, which I did a couple of times. People go to the bars all week and then hit the frats on the weekends. It is fun, but **the bars are pretty small**. They also ID pretty easily, so you don't need a great fake."

Q "Bars are good. A lot of people go to them; **the good ones are Buddhist, the Biltmore, and Coupe's**."

Q "I don't think there any clubs, but **the best bars are Coupe's and the Virginian**. The Biltmore is all right, too."

Q "**There are a bunch of bars on the Corner** that students go to, and there are more downtown."

Q "The bars are numerous. **There are only a few clubs; however, there is no need for them** because we have a lot of fraternities and sororities that dispense both booze and opportunities to dance."

Q "Of course, there are lots of bars near campus. My friends that go out dancing say the gay club is the only good one; **it's not too hard to get into**, you just need to know a member."

Q "There are quite a few bars on the Corner, but you will need a fake ID (unless you know the bartender) to get into them. There is the Biltmore, Jabberwocky, and a few more. With all the frats here, though, **clubs and bars are unnecessary**."

The College Prowler Take On...
Nightlife

Students agree there is hardly a club scene in Charlottesville. There is Club 216 off the Downtown Mall, and then there is whatever Washington DC has to offer which is two and a half hours away. The bars that students frequent are, for the most part, located along the Corner. They are fairly easy to get into and lots of fun. There are plenty of special drink nights that students soon memorize at virtually all the bars along the Corner. Sometimes, these bars feel just like the frat parties, though, simply transplanted into a bar setting. The bars along the Downtown Mall seem more grown-up and "real." They are a refreshing break from the frat parties or the Corner bars. In addition, there are almost always parties within the different organizations and activities that people join—these are often the best times.

The typical evolution of a student's nightlife entertainment is to go to frat parties or organization parties for the first two years, and then to hit up bars along the Corner later on. This is not to say that upperclassmen don't attend frat and organization parties—it just happens less frequently. Try out a bunch of different scenes to see what fits you best, and be open to new experiences. This way, no matter how confined and monotonous Charlottesville nightlife seems to be, you'll have tried it all and gotten the most out of it.

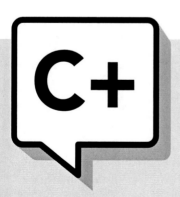

The College Prowler® Grade on
Nightlife: C+

A high grade in Nightlife indicates that there are many bars and clubs in the area that are easily accessible and affordable. Other determining factors include the number of options for the under-21 crowd and the prevalence of house parties.

Greek Life

The Lowdown On...
Greek Life

Number of Fraternities:
32

Undergrad Men in Fraternities:
30%

Number of Sororities:
22

Undergrad Women in Sororities:
30%

➜

Fraternities on Campus:

Alpha Delta Phi
Alpha Epsilon Pi
Alpha Phi Alpha
Alpha Tau Omega
Beta Theta Pi
Chi Phi
Delta Kappa Epsilon
Delta Sigma Phi
Delta Tau Delta
Delta Upsilon
Kappa Alpha
Kappa Sigma
Phi Delta Theta
Phi Gamma Delta
Phi Kappa Psi
Phi Sigma Kappa
Pi Kappa Alpha
Pi Kappa Phi
Pi Lambda Phi
Sigma Alpha Epsilon
Sigma Alpha Mu
Sigma Chi
Sigma Nu
Sigma Phi Epsilon
Sigma Phi
Sigma Pi
St. Anthony Hall
St. Elmo Hall
Theta Chi
Theta Delta Chi
Zeta Beta Tau
Zeta Psi

Sororities on Campus:

Alpha Chi Omega
Alpha Delta Pi
Alpha Omicron Phi
Alpha Phi
Alpha Zeta
Chi Omega
Chi Delta
Delta Delta Delta
Delta Gamma
Delta Zeta
Gamma Phi Beta
Kappa Alpha Theta
Kappa Delta
Kappa Kappa Gamma
Omega Mu
Phi Mu
Pi Beta phi
Sigma Kappa
Sigma Kappa Sigma
Sigma Sigma Sigma
Zeta Tau Alpha
Zeta Tau Gamma

Multicultural Colonies:

Alpha Kappa Delta Phi
(Sorority)
Lambda Upsilon Lambda
(Fraternity)
Lambda Phi Epsilon
(Fraternity)
Lambda Theta Alpha
(Latin Sorority)
Phi Delta Alpha
(Fraternity)

Students Speak Out On...
Greek Life

> **"I had no desire whatsoever to be in a sorority. It may sound cliché, but I don't think its right to buy friends or sisters."**

Q "The Greek life is very popular here, and **it dominates the social scene**, especially for first-years."

Q "Even if you are not associated with the Greek scene, the **culture will likely be thrust upon your life**."

Q "**Two things dominate the social scene: fraternities and bars**. Greek life attracts most first- and second-years, and many third-years. Later in the game, bars become the social stomping grounds. Alcohol is a significant part of the social scene, but it is quite easy to avoid."

Q "Greek life does dominate the social scene—which doesn't mean there aren't other options, but it definitely dominates. **I think, personally, its very superficial**."

Q "**It's enormous**."

Q "At the very least, you should rush. **Rush is nothing but a good thing for guys** (not for girls, though), because you get to do a lot of free, fun stuff and you get to meet a lot of people. There are different social scenes at UVA: non-Greek and Greek. Of course, for me, it feels primarily like a Greek school, since I'm in a fraternity and hang out mainly with other frat brothers."

Q "There are plenty of frats here, but it doesn't dominate the social scene. You will see a ton of people heading to the frats on Thursday and Friday nights, but if you aren't into the Greek life, you will still have a blast. I didn't rush, but only about 40 percent of first-year girls do. **If you are into the Greek life, by all means, go for it**! You'll have a blast and form great relationships."

Q "It's all frats and sororities. After a while, you want to shoot someone because all you see are SUVs. You have to look hard to find people that aren't like this, and then when you do, it's often just people who are consciously trying to be the opposite of a prep, so **they aren't really that interesting**."

Q "It does play a major role at the University, but it does not overwhelm it. **I should add that if you choose to be non-Greek, you are definitely still welcome at parties**; they are not exclusive, and they are all free."

Q "The Greek scene provides fun alternatives to the bar scene, along with dancing. I am biased, though; I am in a frat and love it! I have fun at frat parties, and **if you like to dance, they are usually the best and only bet**."

Q "**Joining a sorority has been one of the best decisions** of my life. However, I have many friends that are not in sororities or frats, and they love their social life."

Q "Greek life is a big part of Virginia social life; however, I'm not Greek, and one doesn't have to become Greek in order to have a good time. **Make sure that if you want to go Greek that it is for you**, because Greek life isn't for everybody."

Q "It's fairly big. **I'm Greek, and I love it**. A lot of my best friends aren't, and they party all the time, so it's not really important. There is a big Greek scene, but you can have just as much fun not being a part of it."

The College Prowler Take On...
Greek Life

Most students feel that Greek life dominates the social scene at UVA. Many are bitter about this, and find it superficial, costly, obnoxious, and over-prevalent. Those involved in Greek life, however, love the people they have met and the relationships they have formed. All sorts of people are involved in the Greek scene, as well as in the non-Greek scene. At UVA, students need to be a bit more open-minded both ways.

On the whole, Greek life only really dominates the campus if you want it to. Of course, fraternities and sororities are a big part of UVA; but keep in mind, this is not the Greek school it once was. At certain times of the academic year, it feels as if the whole school is doing the Greek thing—semi-formals, Foxfield horse races, football games, rush—but when you look closer, you'll see that this is certainly not the case. There are plenty of other groups to join (literary magazines, a cappella groups, theatrical groups, athletic groups, and community service organizations). In any case, even if you don't consider the Greek option, at least go to a frat party at some point— they really can be a fun time, or at least, an interesting experience.

The College Prowler® Grade on
Greek Life: A

A high grade in Greek Life indicates that sororities and fraternities are not only present, but also active on campus. Other determining factors include the variety of houses available and the respect the Greek community receives from the rest of the campus.

Drug Scene

The Lowdown On...
Drug Scene

Most Prevalent Drugs on Campus:

Alcohol

Marijuana

Tobacco

Liquor-Related Referrals:

144

Liquor-Related Arrests:

26

Drug-Related Referrals:

51

Drug-Related Arrests:

9

Drug Counseling
Programs/Substance Abuse Resources

Institute for Substance Abuse Studies – the coordinating body for substance abuse prevention, education, treatment and research at the University (434) 924- 5276.

Peer Health Educators – a peer group trained in substance abuse information providing informal educational sessions (434) 924-1509.

University Police Department – officers providing information and seminars in the legal aspects of areas related to substance abuse
(434) 924-7166.

Consultation and Treatment

Addiction Science Center – outpatient treatment program with free initial evaluation and consultation
(434) 924-0399.

Addiction Treatment Program – inpatient treatment program at Blue Ridge Hospital (434) 924-5555.

Student Health – Alcohol and Substance Abuse Counseling is available from Counseling and Psychological Services for confidential evaluation and treatment of students with substance abuse concerns. Family and group sessions, including groups for ACOAs and recovering students, are also available (434) 924-5556.

Aid to Impaired Residents – information, consultation, intervention, and referrals for Health Sciences Center residents (434) 924-2047.

Assistance on Substance Abuse for Professional Nurses– information, consultation, intervention, and referrals for licensed professional nurses (434) 924-5555.

Students Speak Out On...
Drug Scene

> "There's a lot of alcohol use and abuse, but other drugs aren't as popular. I think 30 percent of students smoke. In my substance abuse class, I think we learned that marijuana was the number one illicit drug used here."

Q "Mostly alcohol, pot, and **a little bit of coke**."

Q "If you don't know about the drug scene, you'll never see it at all. **There are certain sororities and fraternities known for certain drugs**, particularly coke and weed, but that's anywhere you go."

Q "I don't think UVA has a drug problem. Of course, college is a time of experimenting, but **I don't think it's over-indulged at this school**."

Q "People just basically smoke up. **I don't think there is a drug scene**."

Q "I don't know much about the drug scene. I guess if you want to do drugs bad enough you can, but **no one pushes it on you**. To me, it seems nonexistent."

Q "**You can pretty much get whatever you want in town**, but I don't know much about drugs, other than pot. I've heard that the ecstasy here is sketchy, but it's big at Virginia. Alcohol is the main drug that kids use here."

Q "I think it isn't as prevalent as it is at the schools my friends go to, but it is there. Fraternities oftentimes have a good amount of drug use, but it isn't anything that makes me uncomfortable. **I'd say it is average**, maybe less. I don't do any, so I wouldn't know."

Q "I don't know much about drugs. There isn't much, but I guess **it is there if you look hard enough**."

Q "**Of course, weed is available**, but only from a few people. I saw 'X' one time at a rave and never saw the hard stuff. I am very surprised and happy that drug use is not too prevalent. Drinking, on the other hand, is out of hand at UVA!"

Q "Drugs aren't huge, but there is definitely an underground coke scene, which I don't know too much about since I'm not a part of that. **There are some hippies and potheads for good measure, but it's all pretty hidden**."

Q "Drugs are something to definitely stay away from, but I do know that if you want something, **you can get it quite easily**."

The College Prowler Take On...
Drug Scene

Most students don't think of UVA as a drug school. The most-used drug among students is alcohol by far. Generally, if you don't know about drugs or aren't interested in knowing about them, you'll never see the scene around Charlottesville. Some students feel as though marijuana and cocaine are a problem, but for the most part no one sees heavy drug use. Some sororities and fraternities are known for certain drugs, but again, if you don't know about it, you don't see it.

While there definitely are drugs at UVA, the actual scene is a relatively small problem. Essentially, there is a niche for every type of substance, but you'll really have to go looking for any hard drugs. This is something you may run into after a few years in the area, but at first, you're not likely to notice it. In terms of peer pressure, a lot of people don't tend to feel it; while many parties have alcohol, there's little pressure to drink and harder drugs have much less of a presence at student functions. In the end, this school has one of the safer drug scenes around.

B

The College Prowler® Grade on
Drug Scene: B

A high grade in the Drug Scene indicates that drugs are not a noticeable part of campus life; drug use is not visible, and no pressure to use them seems to exist.

Campus
Strictness

The Lowdown On...
Campus Strictness

What Are You Most Likely to Get Caught Doing on Campus?

- Bringing alcohol into the stadium during football games
- Drinking
- Mud sliding
- Parking illegally
- Streaking the lawn

Students Speak Out On...
Campus Strictness

"Whenever I went to football games, I was always surrounded by a bunch of drunks. On several occasions, they got into fights, or sexually harassed the women around them, but the police just ignored it."

Q "They're not at all strict. **They'll drink with you**."

Q "If anything, **they'll just tell you to toss your cup**."

Q "**UVA police are very lenient** when it comes to underage drinking. They realize it's gonna happen."

Q "Drinking is not so bad. There is an organization called Party Patrol that goes around to all of the fraternities on the weekends and tests their enforcement of age restrictions for drinking and other violations (fire traps). They are students, and are therefore, on the whole, more lax than the cops would be—the penalties aren't as steep. **The police generally leave the Frat system alone**. As for drugs, that's a different story. Rumor is, the DEA has an office set up in C-ville and they've made quite a few busts over the years."

Q "As you probably know, Virginia has a reputation for being a party school. **For drinking, just be smart about it**—like, don't walk around with a beer bottle in the dorms around your resident assistant (RA). Other than that, it is pretty lax."

Q "I haven't been caught yet, and **the honor code has a special loophole for drinking**; you don't really get in trouble all that often."

Q "They're not too strict on drinking; it's more like if you are safe, they are happy. **Safety is really their first priority**. As for drugs, I'm not so sure."

Q "Not strict at all. **They're more there to watch out for you than to arrest you**."

Q "They're not strict at all. It's the truth. Well, they are strict if you get caught, but **they're not actively trying to catch people**."

Q "**It's pretty cool**. The resident assistants tend to be stricter, especially if you get one that's a jerk. Smoking needs to be on the down-low, as weed will get you in trouble anywhere."

Q "**I've heard of people getting DUIs** and such, but mostly the police just try to make sure that people are doing okay and that everyone is staying safe."

Q "The campus police are very strict about drugs; if you get caught, you will probably be kicked out. **They understand that college students do drink**, though, and they will warn you first before you get into trouble."

The College Prowler Take On...
Campus Strictness

Students at UVA find that authorities are generally very lenient, especially where alcohol is concerned. In many ways, campus police act more like surrogate parents than strict enforcers; they are mainly concerned with safety, and they are definitely not out to get anyone. RAs and other student security enforcers can be far more strict and obnoxious than the police are, which is the reverse of what you usually find at colleges. If you're caught drinking publicly at UVA, the police are just as likely to ignore it or chuckle and make you toss your cup as they are to actually detain you.

UVA's administration presses down hard on all hard-core drug use, however, and security is more reflective of this. Don't expect security officials to look the same way at drugs as they may at alcohol. The primary goal of UVA security is to keep grounds safe for everyone, and any run-ins you may have will reflect this.

A

The College Prowler® Grade on
Campus Strictness: A

A high Campus Strictness grade implies an overall lenient atmosphere; police and RAs are fairly tolerant, and the administration's rules are flexible.

Parking

The Lowdown On...
Parking

Approximate Parking Permit Cost:
$200 per year

Freshmen Allowed to Park?
No

Student Parking Lot?
Yes (University Hall, dorm parking lots, Scott Stadium)

UVA Parking Services:
Department of Parking & Transportation

(434) 924-7231

www.virginia.edu/parking/faq/faq13.html

Common Parking Tickets:
Expired Meter: $25

No Parking Zone: $30

Handicapped Zone: $100

Fire Lane: $100

Parking Permits

UVA parking permits are only given to faculty, staff, students living on grounds, and the handicapped. Even students living on grounds do not have an easy time of obtaining a permit—you are never guaranteed one. Rather, the permits are given out in sort of a lottery system. If you can't get a permit for your dorm parking lot, then you can most likely get one for U-Hall (the huge parking lot next to the basketball stadium); this isn't terribly helpful, however, as it's far away from most things on grounds. First-year students are not allowed to have a car on grounds until second semester. Even then, you are forced to park in U-Hall—which, again, is almost pointless. You're better off just riding the bus for the first year.

Did You Know?

Best Places to Find a Parking Spot

During the day: the 14th St. parking garage, the parking lot on Elliewood Ave., the Newcomb Hall parking garage, JPA (Jefferson Park Ave.), streets off of Rugby Rd. (Gordon Ave., Grady Ave.). And at night: virtually anywhere!

Good Luck Getting a Parking Spot Here!

Along 14th St., or anywhere along the Corner

Students Speak Out On...
Parking

> "There is not nearly enough parking, currently, but UVA has built and is building more parking garages and expanding some parking lots."

Q "It is not easy to park on campus. You can park in the parking garage or get a pass for U-Hall, but then you will need to take the bus to campus. **The parking patrol is pretty diligent here**, so most of the time you are not going to be able to get away with parking your car in a reserve lot for an hour or so. If you decide to live off campus and you have a car, make sure your apartment has off-street parking. Some of the rental agencies (without off-street parking) will tell you that parking is not a problem, but it usually is unless you have a spot or lot of your own."

Q "Parking sucks. **Ticket ladies are all over**. It's very easy to get towed."

Q "**No, parking is not easy**! If you don't have a parking permit and you try to park somewhere, you're going to get towed. During my third year, I easily racked up over $150 in parking-related fees. (I got three parking tickets and was towed once.)"

Q "I never had a car, so I never had to deal with it. Unless you have a parking pass, **you're out of luck**."

Q "Parking can be a real pain. **The parking cops are horrible, horrible people** who are way too efficient. I lived at a frat house with a parking lot, so I was okay. A lot of apartments offer lot parking, as well, and there's a bunch of street parking off grounds. Watch out if you park somewhere illegally, though!"

Q "Is it easy to park? What a laugh! Parking is atrocious at UVA. First-years are not allowed to bring cars at all anymore, whereas before they were allowed to bring them second semester. Once you are out of your first year, if you are living on grounds, be prepared to fight lottery-style over a parking space for your car to be even somewhat near your dorm. And **when all else fails, be prepared to use University Hall.**"

Q "**You'll have to park at the stadium** and take a bus to school if you drive."

Q "Students can't get a parking permit until sophomore year, and then **they usually have to park it at the basketball arena and get a bus there.** I didn't have a car, but my roommate did. You don't need it that often because there are always buses, but it was nice for going off grounds."

Q "Parking is tough, but everything is within walking distance, so it doesn't really matter. The walking is really not bad. **There are also tons of bus routes.**"

Q "I won't lie, it really sucks. But **the bus system is money**, and my classes were only a five- to ten-minute walk."

Q "**Parking sucks unless you get a pass**. You're not allowed to have a car until second semester, but I wouldn't recommend one until you actually live somewhere that authorizes a spot for you."

The College Prowler Take On...
Parking

Students find that parking anywhere in Charlottesville is pretty atrocious. There aren't enough spaces for the number of cars that are on the road already, and the University population only gets bigger each year. Many students are incredibly frustrated with the steep price of a UVA permit that doesn't even guarantee convenient parking. The rest of Charlottesville is not much better—sometimes finding street parking is easier and safer than trying to park in your own apartment's lot! The parking enforcers are heartless and way too efficient. If you own a car in Charlottesville, then in all likelihood, you will have some sort of parking violation added to your record during your time at school.

Don't even think about driving to class unless you want to pay $1.70 an hour in the bookstore parking garage. Use the bus system, or better yet, just walk; almost everything is within walking distance, anyway. Try to avoid parking illegally, even for just a few minutes, because the parking enforcers will be quick to nab you. Also, be aware that special events, such as football games or graduation, can cause traffic and parking problems throughout all of Charlottesville. If you have a car, it's good to remember these dates and be prepared.

The College Prowler® Grade on

Parking: D

A high grade in this section indicates that parking is both available and affordable, and that parking enforcement isn't overly severe.

Transportation

The Lowdown On...
Transportation

Ways to Get Around Town:

On Campus

There are UVA buses that run all over grounds for free. They come to each bus stop every 10 minutes during the weekdays and every 20 minutes over the weekends and at night. There is also a van escort service that runs at night from 6 p.m. until 7 a.m. You must call ahead from wherever you are, and they come to your door. There is normally a bit of a wait for this service.

(On Campus, continued)

Also, there is a special arrangement that if a student is out at night and too intoxicated to drive home, he/she can take a cab for free and charge it to UVA. Virtually everything you need (with the exception of a grocery store, in some cases) is within walking distance. Check the Web site *www.virginia.edu/parking* for a list of UVA bus schedules.

➜

Public Transportation

Besides the UVA bus system, there are city buses that run all over town. Call (434) 296-7433 or visit www.charlottesville.org for more information.

Also, there is a free trolley that runs from the UVA bus stops to the Downtown Mall every 15 minutes.

Taxi Cabs

A-C Airport/Wahoo Cab
(434) 981-0585

AAA Cab
(434) 975-5555

Abacal
(434) 981-6800

Airport Cab
(434) 295-4131

Cavalier Taxi
(434) 981-5555

Checker Cab Co.
(434) 296-8596

Charlottesville Cab Co.
(434) 981-9594

Rainbow Taxi
(434) 975-5555

Virginia Tours
(434) 293-7598

Yellow Cab
(434) 295-4131

Car Rentals

Avis, local: (434) 973-6000; national: 1-800-831-2847 www.avis.com

Hertz, local: (434) 297-4288; national: 1-800-654-3131 www.hertz.com

(Car Rentals, continued)

National, local: (434) 974-4664; national: 1-800-227-7368 www.nationalcar.com

Best Ways to Get Around Town

Perhaps the best way to get around town is to drive—either have a car, or use a friend for theirs. The buses are convenient, for the most part, but sometimes it is a pain to wait. It's virtually impossible just to hail a taxi cab, unless you're at the airport or train station. Usually, you must call ahead for one.

Ways to Get Out of Town:

There are planes, trains, and all sorts of automobiles, but again, perhaps getting a friend to take you to wherever you want to go would be easiest. If you are friendless, you can call for a taxi or take the shuttle to the airport, or you can try Amtrak or the bus.

Most students have cars or rides to get out of town (airfare is normally pretty pricey out of the Charlottesville airport, and trains and buses can be more time-consuming than necessary). There is a bulletin in Newcomb Hall that advertises for those who have or need rides, and there is often a shuttle bus or carpool that goes up to Northern Virginia, especially for breaks.

Airlines Serving Charlottesville

Delta, 1-800-354-9822
www.delta-air.com

United, 1-800-241-6522
www.united.com

US Airways, 1-800-428-4322
www.usairways.com

Airport

Charlottesville-Albemarle
Airport

(434) 973-8342

www.gocho.com

The airport is about 20-30
minutes from Grounds. It
offers 60 daily non-stop
flights to and from Charlotte,
Pittsburgh, Philadelphia, New
York/LaGuardia, Washington/
Dulles, Cincinnati, and Atlanta.
Because it is such a small
airport, the airfare tends to be
a bit pricey.

How to Get to the Airport

Follow Route 29 North
approximately 8 miles past
Forest Lakes Subdivision and
shopping center on right.
At next intersection turn left
onto Route 649 and follow
Route 649 to a four-way
stop at intersection of State
Routes 649 (Airport Road), 606
(Dickinson Road), and Bowen
Loop Road. Proceed straight
through this intersection onto
Bowen Loop Road, and follow
to air carrier terminal complex.

A cab ride to the airport costs
around $30.

Greyhound

(800) 229-9424

www.greyhound.com

The Greyhound bus station is
located on Main Street on the
right before the Downtown
Mall (10-15 minutes from
grounds, depending on traffic).

Amtrak

(800) USA-RAIL

www.amtrak.com

The Amtrak train station is
located off of Main Street
on the right as you drive
toward the Downtown Mall
(10 minutes from grounds,
depending on traffic).

Travel Agents

Enterprise Travel
400 E Main St.
(434) 296-7500

Globe Travel
1932 Arlington Blvd.
(434) 296-0171

Peace Frogs Travel/Outfitters
1145 Emmet St. N
(434) 977-1415

STA travel
located on the ground floor
of Newcomb Hall
(434) 924-4445

Students Speak Out On...
Transportation

"To get around UVA, it's really simple and free, but to get around town, it's less convenient and actually costs something. The worst is to try to grocery shop without a car."

Q "The UVA bus system is great here, and **you don't really need a car**."

Q "The University buses will take you everywhere you need to go and are pretty regular. The campus is easily walkable, though, whether you live on 14th or Rugby or around the JPA area. There are city buses that run up University Avenue, through the University, and by the hospital. The city buses are really nice and punctual. There is a free trolley that runs to the Downtown Mall every 15 minutes. So all in all, **public transportation is really good and very convenient**."

Q "City buses cost 75 cents (which includes one transfer). Also, if you ride a University bus to the city bus, you can ask the driver for transfers (he gives you two). This is to say that students can usually ride the city buses for free, if they remember to ask for transfers. If you are planning on riding the city bus often, **you can get a book of discounted tickets** (40 for $20) so you then ride for 50 cents. Most city buses will come to a particular stop every hour. The trolley that runs through grounds comes every 15 minutes. Most buses stop running around 6 p.m., but there is limited nighttime service until midnight. The buses are really reliable, and you will never miss a transfer if you ask the driver right away for the transfer ticket."

Q "It sucks. It takes a long time to get certain places, it smells on the bus, and there's always somebody crazy who sits next to you. The solution to this is to **find older friends who have cars**."

Q "**Getting to Barracks Road is possible by bus**, but it takes a good long time, so plan on it. Otherwise, I've never attempted public transportation past the confines of the University area."

Q "Getting around campus is great. Getting around town is not so great. **I prefer to have a car**. Others make due."

Q "There is public transportation that is very convenient, although **it's mostly used to stop students from drinking and driving**."

Q "**Public transportation will take you anywhere**. Between buses and escort services, it's great."

Q "**UVA transport is money**. Bring or borrow a car, however, if you live off campus."

Q "The Greyhound station is within a mile, I can get to Amtrak with a 15-minute walk from where I live, and the airport is a 20-minute ride from campus. **All in all, getting places from Charlottesville is pretty easy**."

Q "**Buses run all the time** and are free."

Q "On grounds, the buses are great. I took them everywhere. **It even takes you to one shopping center**."

Q "**The bus system is really convenient**; you won't have a problem there. It will take you a couple of days to get the routes and buses down, though."

The College Prowler Take On...
Transportation

Most students find public transportation around Charlottesville to be pretty reliable, but a bit of a hassle. Once you get the different routes, times, and fares down, the Charlottesville bus system can be easy and convenient—especially if you don't have a car. Buses will take you wherever you need to go, as long as you're prepared to wait a bit and to deal with some strange people along the way. Around grounds, the UVA shuttles are great; they run pretty frequently and are free for students.

Although it's easy to walk almost anywhere on campus, Charlottesville itself is not always a walking town. Getting to a grocery store is one of the most inconvenient things for students, and this is when it's best to use your own car or mooch a ride from friends. After your first year, having a car in Charlottesville will seem very liberating, although between the bus and shuttle system and the downtown trolley, it's really not essential. If you have to rely on public transit, learn the schedules and transfer system as well as you can; it will save you time and money, and make life without a car a whole lot easier.

The College Prowler® Grade on
Transportation: B+

A high grade for Transportation indicates that campus buses, public buses, cabs, and rental cars are readily-available and affordable. Other determining factors include proximity to an airport and the necessity of transportation.

Weather

The Lowdown On...
Weather

Average Temperature:

Fall:	58 °F
Winter:	35 °F
Spring:	56 °F
Summer:	76 °F

Average Precipitation:

Fall:	3.5 in.
Winter:	3.2 in.
Spring:	4.0 in.
Summer:	3.7 in.

Students Speak Out On...
Weather

"It's hot and humid in summer and early fall, and it's rainy in spring—very rainy. Sometimes, we get a lot of snow in the winter, and sometimes, none."

Q "The weather is unpredictable. When it rains, it doesn't stop, and when it doesn't we have a drought. And when it snows, it snows for eight years. **My suggestion: buy a farmer's almanac**."

Q "The only constant about Charlottesville weather is that it's not constant. **The weather varies so much, even over the course of a week**. Make sure you have clothes for every season."

Q "In general, the weather's pretty nice. We get a wide variety, and the seasons are very distinct. **Winters are cold, but summers are hot**."

Q "It varies a lot. Sometimes it's rainy, sometimes hot, and sometimes quite cold. **Bring a wide variety of clothing**, and make sure you can handle the rain."

Q "It is very warm at the beginning of the year in August and September—bring clothes for 90 degrees with high humidity and lots of walking. Then, **in the winter, be prepared for snow**, with your snow boots for walking to classes that are hardly ever cancelled for weather."

Q "Most of the time, **the weather is nice**."

Q "**The weather is psychotic**. We could have a 70-degree day in January, and then it won't be 70 again until, like, May. It's always changing, but it's neat. It keeps things interesting."

Q "I only got one bad winter in four years, which was nice. **The fall and spring are unbelievably beautiful**, with the foliage and blooming, respectively."

Q "The weather here is great! I love it. **Most people seem to love it**. It's mild and warm for many parts of the year."

Q "I think it is fabulous. The spring is gorgeous; the winter is mild and sort of wet. **It was hot in the beginning of the year**, and it didn't get too cold."

Q "It's pretty warm in the summer and spring, but **it gets cold and can snow in winter**."

Q "We have four seasons. **The scenery is beautiful; you will love it**. We invest heavily in our landscaping—that attracts even non-Virginia students."

Q "**It's hot during the summer**, but there's not too much snow in the winter."

Q "We have great seasons—you get the full range of fall, winter, spring, and summer. **It will snow occasionally**, but it doesn't get tiresome."

Q "There are beautiful falls, mild winters, and great springs and summers. **Virginia Beach is nearby**. I have lived here for two years, and I love the weather."

The College Prowler Take On...
Weather

Charlottesville is definitely a four-season town. The winters are frigid, the summers are sweltering, and the autumns and springs are pleasant, but rainy. Most students find the weather unpredictable and varied, but fun and interesting all the same. The falls and springs are probably the most enjoyable parts of the year for UVA students who love being outside.

To give you an example, some years ago, there was a terrible drought over the end of the summer that didn't break until November. The winter that year was filled with sporadic, heavy snows that didn't end until March; the spring was also particularly wet. Given such unpredictable weather, it's best to come prepared with your wardrobe. Have clothes for all seasons on hand, even when it may not be that particular season. Overall, everyone seems to agree that the weather, combined with UVA grounds and scenery, is really very lovely.

The College Prowler® Grade on
Weather: B

A high Weather grade designates that temperatures are mild and rarely reach extremes, that the campus tends to be sunny rather than rainy, and that weather is fairly consistent rather than unpredictable.

Report Card Summary

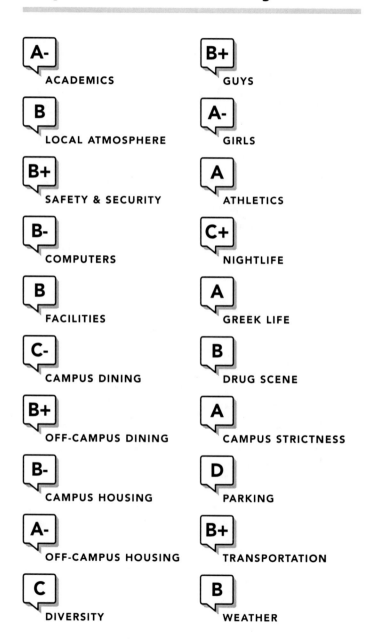

A- ACADEMICS

B+ GUYS

B LOCAL ATMOSPHERE

A- GIRLS

B+ SAFETY & SECURITY

A ATHLETICS

B- COMPUTERS

C+ NIGHTLIFE

B FACILITIES

A GREEK LIFE

C- CAMPUS DINING

B DRUG SCENE

B+ OFF-CAMPUS DINING

A CAMPUS STRICTNESS

B- CAMPUS HOUSING

D PARKING

A- OFF-CAMPUS HOUSING

B+ TRANSPORTATION

C DIVERSITY

B WEATHER

Overall Experience

Students Speak Out On...
Overall Experience

"The school was really great, believe it or not. There's a great party scene. Some find it too preppy, but you can find just about any sort of crowd. I never regretted going to UVA over Duke."

"Because I did not fit in well with the dominant social scene at UVA (Greek-influenced, pretentious . . . shall I go on?), I often thought I would be better suited elsewhere. But if you're in-state, **it's a great deal for the money**, and that is why I stayed."

Q "**I did wish I was somewhere else some of the time**. The best time that I had in college was when I was studying abroad in Spain in the UVA program. UVA is so big, it was hard to connect with a lot of people when there. I recognize that my experience at UVA was not like most, but now that I've graduated, I'm glad I went to UVA. The degree means something—it's a really good school."

Q "I miss college already. I just graduated a month ago and am already envious of my kid brother coming here in the fall. I miss the UVA lifestyle. When I was there, **I never wanted to be anywhere else**."

Q "I miss being around people my own age all the time. It's so hard to meet people out of college, since I left. **I think there are a lot of great colleges in Virginia**, but UVA is definitely the best. There was no question about me being there."

Q "**I love it and can't wait to go back in the fall**. I've been able to keep up with everyone I met this past year so far this summer."

Q "There are great traditions. UVA has some really neat ones; you really end up feeling that you are part of the original scheme that Jefferson thought up. The campus is beautiful, and the memories made here are unique, but this sometimes gives us a reputation for being a snobby school. Other schools think we are too traditional and too Greek. However, **the traditions can be really positive things, too**."

Q "I hate the people here, but I am learning enough that it doesn't matter. And, of course, just like anywhere, **you can find people to hang out with that are like you**."

Q "No way did I ever think about being somewhere else. **I like it here, most of the time**."

Q "**UVA is really big into tradition**. I love the feeling that the University tries to preserve some of the best parts of its past while opening the door to new things everyday. I do not know what else I can say about UVA, other than the fact that it was truly the best four years of my life, and I will be back for many years to come. UVA has one of the world's largest endowments—UVA alumni give back more money than most schools, which I think is a testament to how much they loved their time here!"

Q "**I personally love UVA**. The thing to remember is that you will meet people who will one day become the political, business, and social leaders of the country. When you graduate from UVA, it's like graduating from an Ivy League school, because it feels Ivy League, and there are numerous alumni who are currently CEOs who love to hire UVA students."

Q "I love Virginia! I'm so happy I chose it, and I wouldn't go anywhere else. **I've made great friends, and I have lots of fun**, do well, and learn a lot. I think it's a wonderful community, and there is a lot of school spirit and always plenty to get involved in. For me, it is a perfect mix of academics and fun."

Q "This school has exceeded all my expectations I ever envisioned for college. Basically, **if you're into fraternities and sororities, we definitely have them here**. If you drink, we definitely also have that here. If you do not enjoy that scene, there is always a ton of other stuff to do."

Q "Although I am transferring, I think that UVA is a very good school. I had a lot of fun there, and I did not wish that I was anywhere else this past year. The only reason that I am transferring is because **I am getting more scholarship money**."

Q "UVA is the perfect mix of academic and social elements. I have friends who will wax about Kierkegaard and Emerson, and then five hours later they'll bong beers and slow dance. Basically, there is no better place to experience it all. If you want to immerse yourself in a difficult and complex academic world, then it is possible—the professors are brilliant and prominent. If you want to go to frat parties, football games, bars, and formals, then you can do that, as well. Plus, **the campus is probably the most beautiful one around**."

Q "This place is nice, once you get used to it. I have major culture shock coming here from Miami. Anyhow, I had a great time here but I would like to point out my main criticism: people here live in a bubble and are generally naive. This place lacks street smarts completely. It's a bubble of people who believe in an ideal world that doesn't exist. Here's what's good about the school: it's amazingly beautiful, **and there's lots of beautiful stuff** to do. When you get here, people will not be as mature as you are; about two-thirds of the school is from Northern VA, so they will all be coming from the same high school. There isn't much creativity here beyond the drama department, and ironically, we have one of the best and toughest English programs."

The College Prowler Take On...
Overall Experience

Most students talk about the wonderful experiences and positive feelings they associate with UVA; the University has some of the most devoted alumni in the country. Of course, there are those who wished they had gone somewhere else, and those who were turned off by things such as the lack of diversity, the prominence of Greek life, student naïvety, or the pretentiousness that is, in fact, present on grounds. Those who really like UVA appreciate its traditions, the friendly and outgoing atmosphere, the beautiful setting, and the outstanding academic environment. Students definitely have their share of rough, sad, aggravating moments at UVA. When all is said and done, however, many claim that they couldn't imagine being anywhere else. There are so many different experiences here—putting together an unorganized, student-run play with remarkable, self-motivated students, studying abroad, drinking wine and chatting with a favorite professor in his/her home, tutoring at a local school, or sunning out on the lawn with friends—that, in the end, are some of the many reasons why students are happy at UVA.

If you come to UVA, be prepared to take the good with the bad. In my view, the positive aspects of the University outweigh the negatives, and the environment is as vibrant and intelligent as it was when Thomas Jefferson founded it, well over a century ago.

The Inside Scoop

The Lowdown On...
The Inside Scoop

Things I Wish I Knew Before Coming to UVA

- Definitely live in the old dorms for at least a year—they are more social and friendly.

- Even if you don't get into the classes you want during summer orientation, do not fear, you can always try to get in during the first week of classes.

Tips to Succeed at UVA

- It is important to be friendly and open to anyone and anything.

- Be eager and persistent about doing the things that you want; don't be intimidated by the crowds.

- There is so much opportunity at UVA—don't be afraid to grab it.

UVA Urban Legends

There are plenty of UVA myths floating around. One is that Dr. Seuss used to live in this great big house up on the hill, looking down towards Newcomb Hall. Apparently, after being rejected from UVA, he wrote a little book called *How the Grinch Stole Christmas*. In this book, he depicted himself as the grouchy, resentful old Grinch staring down at all the "Whos in Whoville." Another myth—a bit more racy—is that any first-year girl who walks across the big white Z letters painted all around grounds (which signify the "Z" secret society) will get pregnant. Still another that is re-ignited every year as the entering class settles in is that, in the first weekend students are in town, Dave Matthews supposedly plays an all-day concert in the amphitheater. Don't be a poor sap and wait all-day long by yourself in the amphitheater! I can pretty much guarantee he won't show.

School Spirit

UVA has great school spirit, especially at football and basketball games, where among other things you can find bodies spray-painted in orange and blue, girls dressed in their best pearls, and guys wearing orange bowties. Students at Virginia are incredibly proud of their school and like to go all-out for spirit events. In a school so thick with pride and tradition, there are plenty of opportunities to show support.

Traditions

• The Dressing up for football games and singing the "Good Ole' Song" after every UVA touchdown.

• Spending time on the Lawn on beautiful days.

• Camping out for the Duke vs. UVA football game.

• Painting Beta Bridge late night/early morning.

• Eating at Little John's at 4 a.m.

• Foxfield horse races.

• Streaking the Lawn.

Finding a Job or Internship

The Lowdown On...
Finding a Job or Internship

The best way to find anything is to use your connections. The UVA Career Services Center (located on the first floor of Bryant Hall—the football stadium) is very helpful.

Advice

Use Career Services. Check with them early on in your job/ internship search, stop in frequently, and be persistent about getting what you want. The opportunities are available, but sometimes, you'll have to push to get the resources you need.

Career Center Resources & Services

University Career ServicesByrant Hall at Scott Stadium
www.virginia.edu/career
(434) 924-8900
Hours: Monday–Friday 8 a.m.–5 p.m.

The Career Services Center is a Godsend. They can set you up with an externship during the summer, or any other school break, for that matter. They also have internship programs and on-Grounds interviewing available. Their Web site, too, is fantastic. Many students choose to look for jobs through "Hoostrak" (basically Monstertrak), which you sign up for through Career Services. There are plenty of workshops, programs, and recruitments that Career Services host (a week-long career fair, New York City Recruiting Alliance, workshops on creating a nice resume or coverletter and managing your finances post-graduation, mock interviews, etiquette classes, counseling, etc.). Career Services also provides plenty of information on graduate schools, law school, any sort of continuing education, as well as fellowships, teaching English abroad, and essentially any other possible career choice. Finally, the people there are fantastic—knowledgeable, helpful, and most importantly, friendly.

Alumni

The Lowdown On...
Alumni

Office:
The UVA Alumni Association is located in Alumni Hall at 211 Emmet Street South, across the street from the University's Memorial Gymnasium.

Web Site:
www.alumni.virginia.edu

Services Available:
Career Services Center

Cavaliers Care (nationwide volunteerism initiative)

Clubs (in every state)

Interest Groups (Asian & Asian Pacific American Alumni Network)

Student Programs (4th Year Trustees, Class Councils, funding/creating Jefferson Scholarships)

Young Alumni Council

Average Salary Information

College of Arts and Sciences:

Advertising/Marketing	$25,000-$35,000
Banking	$35,000-$60,000
Biotech/Pharmaceuticals/Medical Devices	$28,000-$40,500
Communications/Media	$22,000-$35,000
Education	$21,000-$38,788
Environment	$28,000-$33,009
Government/Public Administration	$26,000-$49,000
Healthcare	$22,173-$31,500
Insurance	$34,000-$36,000
Legal/Law Enforcement	$24,000-$32,000

Engineering School

Aerospace Engineering	$44,745
Applied Math	$43,000
Chemical Engineering	$48,223
Civil Engineering	$43,228
Computer Engineering	$54,000
Computer Science	$54,200
Electrical Engineering	$54,000
Engineering Physics	$52,000
Mechanical Engineering	$48,800
Systems and Information Engineering	$50,000

Commerce School

Accounting	$43,267
Consulting	$47,241
Finance	$49,336
Human Resources Management	$39,667
Information Systems	$47,171
Marketing Sales	$37,511
Operations	$44,000

Major Alumni Events

Fourth Year special events

Parties/Gatherings in major cities

Reunions

Sponsorship of Jefferson Scholars

Tailgates

Did You Know?

Famous UVA Alumni

Edgar Allan Poe (Attended 1826–1827; did not graduate) – Famous poet/writer

Woodrow Wilson (Attended 1879) – Famous, idealistic politician; former president of the US; founder of League of Nations; Nobel Prize laureate

Stanley Winston (Class of 1968) – Motion picture special effects expert

Katie Couric (Class of 1979) – News anchor on the *Today Show* (NBC)

Valerie B. Ackerman (Class of 1981) – President and founder of Women's National Basketball Association

Tina Fey (Class of 1992) – Comedian, head-writer, and actor on *Saturday Night Live*

Thomas Jones (Class of 1999) – Running back, Chicago Bears

For more, check out *www.virginia.edu/notablealumni*

Student Organizations

During the first week of school, there will be an activities fair in the amphitheater where you can learn about all the different organizations and even sign up for a few. If ever there seems to be something lacking, many take the initiative to start their own club—this is perhaps the reason why there are so many organizations already at UVA. For an updated list of student organizations, as well as Web links, visit the UVA Student Council's site at *www.uvastudentcouncil.com/ciocentral*

A-Cappella

Abundant Life
Christmas Banquet

Academic Competition Club

Action for a Better Living
Environment (ABLE)

Adventist Christian Fellowship

Afghan Student Association

Agape Christian Fellowship

Albemarle County Foosball
Association

All Student Fellowship

Allure Dance Team

Alpha Chi Sigma

Alpha Epsilon Delta – National
Premedical Honor Society

Alpha Kappa Psi

Alpha Phi Omega

Alpha Psi Epsilon

Alternative Spring Break

American Advertising
Federation

American Forensics Association
at UVA

American Institute of
Aeronautics and Astronautics
(AIAA)

American Institute of
Architecture Students

American Institute of Chemical Engineers

American Red Cross Club at UVA

American Society of Civil Engineers

Amnesty International at UVA

Anthropology Society

Archery Club at University of Virginia

Armenian Cultural Society

Art of Living Club

Art of Living Foundation

Art Students Society

Asian Fraternal League at Virginia

Asian Pacific American Law Students Association

Asian Student Union

Association for Computing Machinery

Association of Student Firefighters at the University of Virginia

AWAKE

Bahai Association

Ballroom Dance Club at UVA

Baptist Student Union

Belly Dance Club at UVA

Best Buddies

Beta Alpha Psi

Bhakti-Yoga Club

Bioethics Society

Biology Society

Biomedical Engineering Society

Black Business Student Forum (BBSF)

Black Commerce Student Network

Black Expression Awareness and Thought Society (BEATS)

Black Fraternal Council

Black Graduate and Professional Student Organization

Black Law Students Association

Black Student Alliance

Black Voices

Blue Notes

Blue Ridge Mountain Rescue Group

Brazilian Jiu-Jitsu Club

Bridge Club

Brothers United Celebrating Knowledge and Success

Buddhist Meditation Society

Building ACROSS

Bulgarian Student Association

Burmese Interact Club

Business Ethics Group

Business Technology Club

C-ville Live

CAINE

Cambodian Student Organization

Campaign for Dance

Campus for Choice

Campus Girl Scouts

Caribbean Student Association

Catholic Student Ministry

Cavalier Association of Vehicles

Cavalier Cardplayer Club

Cavalier Judo Club

Cavalier Life

Cavalier Road Runners

Cavs for Kerry

Cellar Rebellion

Chabad Jewish Heritage Students Association

Chess Club

Chi Alpha Christian Fellowship

Child Relief & You (CRY)

Children of War

Chinese Christian Fellowship

Chinese Medicine Forum

Chinese Student Association

Chinese Students and Scholars Society

CHoosE (Christian Hoos Exalt)

Christian Students on Grounds at UVA

Cigar Society at UVA

Circle K

Classical Liberal Roundtable

Clowns on Grounds

Club Baseball at UVA

Club Softball

Co-Operative Housing at UVA

Cognitive Science Society

College Campaign for Organ Donation

College Republicans

College Student Interest Group in Neurology (CO-SIGN)

Collegiate Mock Trial

Colombian Society

Community Arts Volunteers

Competing Hoos In Mechanical Engineering

Conference on Public Service and the Law

Consortium of University Publications

Coptic Club

Corks & Curls

Cycling Club

Dance Marathon at the University of Virginia

Daniel Hale Williams Pre-Med/ Pre-Dental Society

Darden African Business Organization

Darden Christian Fellowship

Darden Consulting Club

Darden Energy Club

Darden Health Care Club

Darden Jewish Student Association

Darden Private Equity Network

Darden Real Estate Club

Darden Rowing Club

Deafness Education and Awareness For all Students

Disciples of Bob Barker

Dolci

Eastern Films Appreciation Club

Eco House Initiative

Ektaal

Embrace Diversity

Engineering Students Without Borders

Entrepreneurs & Venture Capital Club

Environmental Law Forum

Environmental Sciences Organization

ETA Lodge

Etcetera Winterguard

European Society

European Society at Darden

Extreme Paper Challenge

F.O.R.C.E.

Fashion Design Club

FBLA-Phi Beta Lambda at the University of Virginia

Federalist Society

Fellowship of Christian Athletes

FilmMaker's Studio

First Right

First Year Fellowship

First Year Players

Fly Fishing Club at UVA

Four-Square Club

Free the Children International

Gaining Understanding Through Support (GUTS)

Gamers

GEMS

General Management and Operations Club

Global Public Health Society

Grace Christian Fellowship

Graduate Law Students Association

Graduate Religious Studies Association

Graduate Women in Business

Greek Jewish Council

H.O.P.E. (Hoos Open to Preventing Eating Disorders)

Habitat for Humanity

Health Law Interest Group

Health Unity Council

Hellenic Society

Hillel Jewish Student Union

Hindu Students Council

Hispamérica Graduate and Professional Student Organization at UVA

Hispanic American Network at Darden

History Club

HK Cinema

Hong Kong Students Association

Hoos Against Single Sanction

Hoos Aware

Hoos for Howard Dean

Hoos for Israel

Hoos for Lieberman

Hoos for Wesley Clark

Hoos in Treble

Hoos on a Budget

Hoos Perspective

Hoos Sober

Hullabahoos

Human Rights Study Project

Impact Movement

Indian Student Association

Individual Rights Coalition

Inkstone Literary Magazine

Inter-Fraternity Council

International Business Society – Darden

International Justice Mission Campus Chapter at UVA

International Relations Organization

International Students Admission Committee (ISAC)

InterVarsity Christian Fellowship

ISKF Karate at the University of Virginia

Italian Society

Ivanhoe Road

J.B. Moore Society of International Law

Japanese Club

Jefferson Leadership Foundation

Jefferson Literary and Debating Society

Jewish Law Students Association

John Edwards Cavaliers

Journal of Law and Politics

Jubilate

Kids Acting Out

Korean Catholic Student Ministry

Korean Graduate Student Association (KOGSA)

Korean Student Association

Kriya

Kumdo Club at UVA

Lambda Law Alliance

LASA – Latin Student Association

Latino Student Union

Latino Student Union

Law Christian Fellowship

Law Partners

Law School Mock Trial

Lax Lite

Legal Assistance Society

Libel Show

LMNTal

Local Tea

Lutheran Student Movement

Madison House

Mahogany Dance Troupe

Malaysian Students Association (MSA-UVA)

March of Dimes Collegiate Council

Marketing Club at Darden

Materials Science & Engineering Graduate Student Board

McIntire Hospitality Group

McIntire Marketing Association

McIntire Women\'s Business Forum

Medart

Media, Entertainment and Sports Club

Medical Supplies Mission

Men's Club Lacrosse

Men's Ice Hockey Club

Men's Club Soccer

Military Association at Darden (MAD)

Minority Rights Advocacy Coalition

Model International House of Pancakes

Monroe Society

Mountain Bike Club at UVA

Multiracial Student Union

Musicians On Call

Muslim Students Association

National Association of Black Accountants, Inc.

National Lawyers Guild--UVA Chapter

National Organization for Women at UVA

National Society of Black Engineers

National Society of Collegiate Scholars

Native American Student Union

NatureSpirit at UVA

Net Impact at McIntire

Net-Impact at Darden

OFF THE LAWN

OFFScreen

Oliver Hill Pre-Law Society

Oluponya Records

Olympiclifting and Powerlifting Team

Omicron Delta Kappa

One in Four

Operation Smile

Organization of African Students

Organization of Black Chemist and Chemical Engineers

Organization of Young Filipino Americans

Orthodox Christian Fellowship

Out On Rugby

Outdoors at UVA

O'Tones

Pakistan Students League

Patrick Henry Law Society

Pause

Perfect Praise Dance Ministries

Persian Cultural Society

Phi Alpha Delta Pre-Law Fraternity

Phi Delta Phi, Minor Inn

Phi Eta Sigma Honor Society

Phi Sigma Pi

Polish American Students Association

Practically Speaking

Pre-Dental Society

Pre-Vet Society

Pro Bono Criminal Assistance Project

Promoting -HIV- Negativity

Public Interest Law Association

Quaker Worship Group at UVA

Queer Christian Fellowship

Queer Student Union

R.O.C.K. S.T.A.R.

Rag & Bone

Random Acts of Kindness

Rape Crisis Advocacy Project

Reformed University Fellowship

Relay for Life

Remix

Rex E. Lee Law Society

Rhapsody Dance Ensemble

Romanian Society

Sailing Association at UVA

SAVE

SDC Investment Club

SDC Investments

Semper Fidelis Society

Sexual Assault Facts and Education

Sexual Assault Peer Advocacy

Shades of Expression

Shakespeare on the Lawn

Sharaara

SHOUT (Student Health OUTreach)

Siebzehns

Sigma Psi Zeta

Sikh Students Association

Silver Wings

Simchah

Singapore Student Association

Society of Hispanic Professional Engineers

Society of Tournament Players

Society of Women Engineers

Solar Car Team

South Asian Leadership Society

Special Friends

Spectrum Theatre

Spic Macay

St. Thomas More Society

Step It Up

Street Addicts

Strike Out Muscular Dystrophy

Student Association of Landscape Architects

Student Docent Program at UVA

Student Environmental Action

Student Legal Forum

Student Planners Association

Student Pugwash

Student Theatre Alliance

Student Virginia Education Association

Student Watch at UVA

Students for a Free Tibet

Students for Animal Rights

Students for Clark, UVA Chapter

Students for Creative Anachronism

Students for Individual Liberty

Students for Peace and Justice in Palestine

Students for Sustainable Communities

Students for the Second Amendment

Students Promoting Fair Trade

Students Taking A Stand

Students Teaching, Educating, and Preparing Students (STEPS)

Students United for Progressive Change

Study Abroad Club

Sullen Art Society of Creative Writers

SUR

Surf Club

Sustained Dialogue

Swing Club at UVA

Table Tennis Club

Tae Kwon Do Club at UVA

Taiwanese Student Association

Tea Club

Team Cavalier

Thai Students Organization

The Academical Village People

The Aikido Club at UVA

The American Constitution Society for Law and Policy

The Arab Student Organization

The Asian Business Club at Darden

The Assemblage of Cain

The Boogie Club

The Cavalier Daily

The Christian Science Organization at UVA

The Classics Club at UVA

The Darden Follies

The Declaration

The Ellison Society

The English Club

The Garage at UVA

The German Society

The Griot Society

The Jugglers Guild at the University of Virginia

The Korean Studies Organization

The Liberty Coalition

The Myo Sim Karate Club at UVA

The New Dominions

The Organization of Bangladeshi Students

The Red Brick Society

The Scuba Club at the University of Virginia

The Sky Club at Darden

The Songwriting Society of UVA

The Tastemasters of Virginia

The University Fight Club for Boxing and Kickboxing

The Virginia Gentlemen

The Virginia Literary Review

TheCompoundWord

Theta Tau

Thomas Jefferson Chapter of the Society of Architecture

Thomas Jefferson Chapter of the Society of Architectural Historians

Thursday Night Praise and Worship

Tires & Axles: VA Offroad

Towards a Better Latin America (TBLA)

Trigon Engineering Society

Turkish Society at UVA

Tyrannosaurus Rock

Uechi-ryu Karate Club

Undergraduate Writers Support Network

UNICEF-UVA

Unite for Sight

United Students Against Sweatshops at UVA

University Dance Club

University Democrats

University Free Press

University Giving Tree

University Libertarians

UVA Law School Ambulance Chasers

V.U.U.S. (Virginia Unitarian Universalist Students)

Vietnamese Student Association

Virginia Men's Ultimate Frisbee Club

Virginia Advertising

Virginia Advocate, The

Virginia Alpine Ski Team (VAST)

Virginia Atheist Association

Virginia Belles

Virginia Billiards Club

Virginia Club Badminton

Virginia Club Golf

Virginia Club Men\'s Volleyball

Virginia Diving Club

Virginia Employment and Labor Law Association

Virginia Entrepreneur Organization

Virginia Environmental Law Journal

Virginia Field Hockey Club

Virginia Glee Club

Virginia Grounds Rescue Squad at UVA

Virginia Gymnastics Club

Virginia Irish Society

Virginia Journal of International Law

Virginia Journal of Law & Technology Association

Virginia Journal of Social Policy and the Law

Virginia Law and Business Society

Virginia Law and Graduate Republicans

Virginia Law Families

Virginia Law Veterans

Virginia Law Weekly

Virginia Law Women

Virginia Men's Club Tennis

Virginia Men's Rugby Club

Virginia Pep Band

Virginia Photography Club

Virginia Polo

Virginia Rifle and Pistol Club

Virginia Rowing Association

Virginia Rugby Football Club

Virginia Service Coalition

Virginia Show Choir

Virginia Sil'hooettes

Virginia Snowboard Club

Virginia Society for Recruitment of Scholars

Virginia Society of Law and Technology

Virginia Sports & Entertainment Law Journal

Virginia Squash Team

Virginia Stitch Squad

Virginia Student Transportation Association

Virginia Swimming Club

Virginia Swing Jazz Orchestra

Virginia Tax Review Association

Virginia Transatlantic Society

Virginia Triathlon Club

Virginia Visionaries Association

Virginia Water Polo Club

Virginia Women's Rugby Football Club

Virginia Women's Chorus

Virginia Women's Club Tennis

Virginia Women's Club Volleyball

Virginia Women's Ultimate Frisbee

Virginia Women's Water Polo

Virginia Wushu Club

Vital Signs

Vox: Voices for Planned Parenthood

Voz Latina

W.I.S.E.: Wahoo Informational Service to the Electorate

Washington Literary Society & Debating Union

WHOO Television

Who's HOO (Twins, Triplets, and Other Multiples)

Wide Awake Productions

William Minor Lile Moot Court Board

Women's Club Soccer

Women's Club Basketball at the University of Virgin...

Women's Ice Hockey Club at UVA

Women's Club Lacrosse

WUVA, Inc.

Young Black Entrepreneurs

Young Composers Society

Young Life Leadership

The Best
& Worst

The Ten **BEST** Things About UVA

1	Beautiful surroundings!
2	Amazing professors and classes
3	Vibrant, outgoing people
4	Fun social scene
5	Excellent athletic facilities
6	Incredibly low in-state tuition
7	Charlottesville
8	The Corner
9	The University's history and tradition
10	The easygoing lifestyle

The Ten **WORST** Things About UVA

1 The stifling Greek scene

2 The advising system, or lack thereof

3 Parking, or lack thereof

4 Diversity problems such as self-segregation

5 Pretentiousness or naïveté among students

6 High out-of-state tuition

7 Large general and introductory classes

8 TAs who don't speak English

9 Paying to print in the computer labs

10 Having to leave after graduation

Visiting

The Lowdown On...
Visiting

Hotel Information:

Near the University:

Best Western Cavalier Inn
105 Emmet St. N
Charlottesville, VA 22903
(434) 296-5501
Distance from Campus:
On campus
Price Range: $70–$85

The Boar's Head Inn
200 Ednam Drive
Charlottesville, VA 22901
(434) 296-2181
Distance from Campus:
1 mile
Price Range: $130–$145

→

Holiday Inn North
1901 Emmet Street
Charlottesville, VA 22901
(434) 977-7700
Distance from Campus:
1 mile
Price Range: $65–$80

Red Roof Inn
1309 W Main St.
Charlottesville, VA 22903
(434) 295-4333
Distance from Campus:
Less than 1 mile
Price Range: $90–$115

Near Downtown:

200 South Street Inn
200 South St.
Charlottesville, VA 22902
(434) 979-0200
Distance from Campus:
About 1 mile
Price Range: $100–$125

The Omni Hotel
235 W Main St.
Charlottesville, VA 22902
(434) 971-5500
Distance from Campus:
Less than 1 mile
Price Range: $125–$140

Take a Campus Virtual Tour

An online tour of the residence halls (which aren't shown on the walking tour) can be found at *www.virginia.edu/dorms*

Campus Tours

www.virginia.edu/undergradadmission/schedule.html

Overnight Visits

UVA doesn't generally offer overnight visits for prospective students. It's best if you know someone who is already living in the dorms and can stay with him/her.

Just show up for a tour. There is no need to reserve a space on a tour or in an information session. You may want to call ahead (434) 982-3200 or check the Web site to find out where they will be held, as they can vary. If all else fails, simply show up at Peabody Hall (the admissions building) a little beforehand.

Directions to Campus

The University of Virginia is located in Charlottesville, VA, near the intersection of I-64 and US-29.

From I-64

- Take exit 118B onto the 29/250 Bypass.
- Take the second exit (250 East Business), making a right at the top of the ramp.
- Make another right about a mile later, onto Emmet Street.
- The University will be on your right.

From US-29

- Follow the signs to Business 29, which becomes Emmet Street.
- To reach US-29 from the Northeast, take I-495 around Washington to I-66 West.
- From I-66 West, take the exit marked "US-29 South– Gainesville."
- Follow 29 South for about an hour and a half.
- Make a left onto Emmet Street.
- The University will be on your left.

Words to Know

Academic Probation – A suspension imposed on a student if he or she fails to keep up with the school's minimum academic requirements. Those unable to improve their grades after receiving this warning can face dismissal.

Beer Pong/Beirut – A drinking game involving cups of beer arranged in a pyramid shape on each side of a table. The goal is to get a ping pong ball into one of the opponent's cups by throwing the ball or hitting it with a paddle. If the ball lands in a cup, the opponent is required to drink the beer.

Bid – An invitation from a fraternity or sorority to 'pledge' (join) that specific house.

Blue-Light Phone – Brightly-colored phone posts with a blue light bulb on top. These phones exist for security purposes and are located at various outside locations around most campuses. In an emergency, a student can pick up one of these phones (free of charge) to connect with campus police or a security escort.

Campus Police – Police who are specifically assigned to a given institution. Campus police are typically not regular city officers; they are employed by the university in a full-time capacity.

Club Sports – A level of sports that falls somewhere between varsity and intramural. If a student is unable to commit to a varsity team but has a lot of passion for athletics, a club sport could be a better, less intense option. Even less demanding, intramural (IM) sports often involve no traveling and considerably less time.

Cocaine – An illegal drug. Also known as "coke" or "blow," cocaine often resembles a white crystalline or powdery substance. It is highly addictive and dangerous.

Common Application – An application with which students can apply to multiple schools.

Course Registration – The period of official class selection for the upcoming quarter or semester. Prior to registration, it is best to prepare several back-up courses in case a particular class becomes full. If a course is full, students can place themselves on the waitlist, although this still does not guarantee entry.

Division Athletics – Athletic classifications range from Division I to Division III. Division IA is the most competitive, while Division III is considered to be the least competitive.

Dorm – A dorm (or dormitory) is an on-campus housing facility. Dorms can provide a range of options from suite-style rooms to more communal options that include shared bathrooms. Most first-year students live in dorms. Some upperclassmen who wish to stay on campus also choose this option.

Early Action – An application option with which a student can apply to a school and receive an early acceptance response without a binding commitment. This system is becoming less and less available.

Early Decision – An application option that students should use only if they are certain they plan to attend the school in question. If a student applies using the early decision option and is admitted, he or she is required and bound to attend that university. Admission rates are usually higher among students who apply through early decision, as the student is clearly indicating that the school is his or her first choice.

Ecstasy – An illegal drug. Also known as "E" or "X," ecstasy looks like a pill and most resembles an aspirin. Considered a party drug, ecstasy is very dangerous and can be deadly.

Ethernet – An extremely fast Internet connection available in most university-owned residence halls. To use an Ethernet connection properly, a student will need a network card and cable for his or her computer.

Fake ID – A counterfeit identification card that contains false information. Most commonly, students get fake IDs with altered birthdates so that they appear to be older than 21 (and therefore of legal drinking age). Even though it is illegal, many college students have fake IDs in hopes of purchasing alcohol or getting into bars.

Frosh – Slang for "freshman" or "freshmen."

Hazing – Initiation rituals administered by some fraternities or sororities as part of the pledging process. Many universities have outlawed hazing due to its degrading, and sometimes dangerous, nature.

Intramurals (IMs) – A popular, and usually free, sport league in which students create teams and compete against one another. These sports vary in competitiveness and can include a range of activities—everything from billiards to water polo. IM sports are a great way to meet people with similar interests.

Keg – Officially called a half-barrel, a keg contains roughly 200 12-ounce servings of beer.

LSD – An illegal drug, also known as acid, this hallucinogenic drug most commonly resembles a tab of paper.

Marijuana – An illegal drug, also known as weed or pot; along with alcohol, marijuana is one of the most commonly-found drugs on campuses across the country.

Major –The focal point of a student's college studies; a specific topic that is studied for a degree. Examples of majors include physics, English, history, computer science, economics, business, and music. Many students decide on a specific major before arriving on campus, while others are simply "undecided" until declaring a major. Those who are extremely interested in two areas can also choose to double major.

Meal Block – The equivalent of one meal. Students on a meal plan usually receive a fixed number of meals per week. Each meal, or "block," can be redeemed at the school's dining facilities in place of cash. Often, a student's weekly allotment of meal blocks will be forfeited if not used.

Minor – An additional focal point in a student's education. Often serving as a complement or addition to a student's main area of focus, a minor has fewer requirements and prerequisites to fulfill than a major. Minors are not required for graduation from most schools; however some students who want to explore many different interests choose to pursue both a major and a minor.

Mushrooms – An illegal drug. Also known as "'shrooms," this drug resembles regular mushrooms but is extremely hallucinogenic.

Off-Campus Housing – Housing from a particular landlord or rental group that is not affiliated with the university. Depending on the college, off-campus housing can range from extremely popular to non-existent. Students who choose to live off campus are typically given more freedom, but they also have to deal with possible subletting scenarios, furniture, bills, and other issues. In addition to these factors, rental prices and distance often affect a student's decision to move off campus.

Office Hours – Time that teachers set aside for students who have questions about coursework. Office hours are a good forum for students to go over any problems and to show interest in the subject material.

Pledging – The early phase of joining a fraternity or sorority, pledging takes place after a student has gone through rush and received a bid. Pledging usually lasts between one and two semesters. Once the pledging period is complete and a particular student has done everything that is required to become a member, that student is considered a brother or sister. If a fraternity or a sorority would decide to "haze" a group of students, this initiation would take place during the pledging period.

Private Institution – A school that does not use tax revenue to subsidize education costs. Private schools typically cost more than public schools and are usually smaller.

Prof – Slang for "professor."

Public Institution – A school that uses tax revenue to subsidize education costs. Public schools are often a good value for in-state residents and tend to be larger than most private colleges.

Quarter System (or Trimester System) – A type of academic calendar system. In this setup, students take classes for three academic periods. The first quarter usually starts in late September or early October and concludes right before Christmas. The second quarter usually starts around early to mid–January and finishes up around March or April. The last academic quarter, or "third quarter," usually starts in late March or early April and finishes up in late May or Mid-June. The fourth quarter is summer. The major difference between the quarter system and semester system is that students take more, less comprehensive courses under the quarter calendar.

RA (Resident Assistant) – A student leader who is assigned to a particular floor in a dormitory in order to help to the other students who live there. An RA's duties include ensuring student safety and providing assistance wherever possible.

Recitation – An extension of a specific course; a review session. Some classes, particularly large lectures, are supplemented with mandatory recitation sessions that provide a relatively personal class setting.

Rolling Admissions – A form of admissions. Most commonly found at public institutions, schools with this type of policy continue to accept students throughout the year until their class sizes are met. For example, some schools begin accepting students as early as December and will continue to do so until April or May.

Room and Board – This figure is typically the combined cost of a university-owned room and a meal plan.

Room Draw/Housing Lottery – A common way to pick on-campus room assignments for the following year. If a student decides to remain in university-owned housing, he or she is assigned a unique number that, along with seniority, is used to determine his or her housing for the next year.

Rush – The period in which students can meet the brothers and sisters of a particular chapter and find out if a given fraternity or sorority is right for them. Rushing a fraternity or a sorority is not a requirement at any school. The goal of rush is to give students who are serious about pledging a feel for what to expect.

Semester System – The most common type of academic calendar system at college campuses. This setup typically includes two semesters in a given school year. The fall semester starts around the end of August or early September and concludes before winter vacation. The spring semester usually starts in mid-January and ends in late April or May.

Student Center/Rec Center/Student Union – A common area on campus that often contains study areas, recreation facilities, and eateries. This building is often a good place to meet up with fellow students; depending on the school, the student center can have a huge role or a non-existent role in campus life.

Student ID – A university-issued photo ID that serves as a student's key to school-related functions. Some schools require students to show these cards in order to get into dorms, libraries, cafeterias, and other facilities. In addition to storing meal plan information, in some cases, a student ID can actually work as a debit card and allow students to purchase things from bookstores or local shops.

Suite – A type of dorm room. Unlike dorms that feature communal bathrooms shared by the entire floor, suites offer bathrooms shared only among the suite. Suite-style dorm rooms can house anywhere from two to ten students.

TA (Teacher's Assistant) – An undergraduate or grad student who helps in some manner with a specific course. In some cases, a TA will teach a class, assist a professor, grade assignments, or conduct office hours.

Undergraduate – A student in the process of studying for his or her bachelor's degree.

ABOUT THE AUTHOR

Having just recently graduated from the University of Virginia with a BA in English, it has been a pleasure for me to reflect on my college experience as a whole and share that with you in this book. I know much of it, in fact most of it, is incredibly subjective, but perhaps that is the best way for you to truly get a taste of any place. So in this book, I give you my (as well as many other students') very personal experiences at UVA—by all means, take them in and learn from them.

Since writing this guidebook, I am enjoying life as a writer at the international conservation organization, the Nature Conservancy. I often think back on my days as a student and wish I was still there in Charlottesville. So, enjoy it while you can—there may never be another time in your life with as much absolute freedom and inspiration.

And now, as I close these words and the final chapter of my college career, I am sad and excited. I take with me my writing and my thriving memories of Virginia, and I wish that you, potential students of Virginia, will come to love this place as much as I have.

I thank everyone and everything that went into making this book possible. If you have any questions, comments, or words of flattery, please contact me by e-mail.

Miriam M. Nicklin
miriam@collegeprowler.com.

California Colleges

California dreamin'?
This book is a must have for you!

CALIFORNIA COLLEGES
7¼" X 10", 762 Pages Paperback
$29.95 Retail
1-59658-501-3

Stanford, UC Berkeley, Caltech—California is home
to some of America's greatest institutes of higher
learning. *California Colleges* gives the lowdown on 24
of the best, side by side, in one prodigious volume.

New England Colleges

Looking for peace in the Northeast?
Pick up this regional guide to New England!

NEW ENGLAND COLLEGES
7¼" X 10", 1015 Pages Paperback
$29.95 Retail
1-59658-504-8

New England is the birthplace of many prestigious universities, and with so many to choose from, picking the right school can be a tough decision. With inside information on over 34 competive Northeastern schools, *New England Colleges* provides the same high-quality information prospective students expect from College Prowler in one all-inclusive, easy-to-use reference.

Schools of the South

Headin' down south? This book will help you find your way to the perfect school!

SCHOOLS OF THE SOUTH
7¼" X 10", 773 Pages Paperback
$29.95 Retail
1-59658-503-X

Southern pride is always strong. Whether it's across town or across state, many Southern students are devoted to their home sweet home. *Schools of the South* offers an honest student perspective on 36 universities available south of the Mason-Dixon.

Untangling the Ivy League

The ultimate book for everything Ivy!

UNTANGLING THE IVY LEAGUE
7¼" X 10", 567 Pages Paperback
$24.95 Retail
1-59658-500-5

Ivy League students, alumni, admissions officers, and other top insiders get together to tell it like it is. *Untangling the Ivy League* covers every aspect—from admissions and athletics to secret societies and urban legends—of the nation's eight oldest, wealthiest, and most competitive colleges and universities.

Need Help Paying For School?

Apply for our scholarship!

College Prowler awards thousands of dollars a year to students who compose the best essays. E-mail scholarship@collegeprowler.com for more information, or call 1-800-290-2682.

Apply now at ***www.collegeprowler.com***

Tell Us What Life Is Really Like at Your School!

Have you ever wanted to let people know what your college is really like? Now's your chance to help millions of high school students choose the right college.

Let your voice be heard.

Check out **www.collegeprowler.com** for more info!

Need More Help?

Do you have more questions about this school? Can't find a certain statistic? College Prowler is here to help. We are the best source of college information out there. We have a network of thousands of students who can get the latest information on any school to you ASAP. E-mail us at info@collegeprowler.com with your college-related questions.

E-Mail Us Your College-Related Questions!

Check out *www.collegeprowler.com* for more details.
1-800-290-2682

Write For Us!
Get published! Voice your opinion.

Writing a College Prowler guidebook is both fun and rewarding; our open-ended format allows your own creativity free reign. Our writers have been featured in national newspapers and have seen their names in bookstores across the country. Now is your chance to break into the publishing industry with one of the country's fastest-growing publishers!

Apply now at ***www.collegeprowler.com***

Contact editor@collegeprowler.com or call 1-800-290-2682 for more details.

Pros and Cons

Still can't figure out if this is the right school for you?
You've already read through this in-depth guide; why not
list the pros and cons? It will really help with narrowing down
your decision and determining whether or not
this school is right for you.

Pros	Cons
....	....
....	....
....	....
....	....
....	....
....	....
....	....
....	....
....	....
....	....
....	....
....	....
....	....

Albion College
Alfred University
Allegheny College
American University
Amherst College
Arizona State University
Auburn University
Babson College
Ball State University
Bard College
Barnard College
Bates College
Baylor University
Beloit College
Bentley College
Binghamton University
Birmingham Southern College
Boston College
Boston University
Bowdoin College
Brandeis University
Brigham Young University
Brown University
Bryn Mawr College
Bucknell University
Cal Poly
Cal Poly Pomona
Cal State Northridge
Cal State Sacramento
Caltech
Carleton College
Carnegie Mellon University
Case Western Reserve
Centenary College of Louisiana
Centre College
Claremont McKenna College
Clark Atlanta University
Clark University
Clemson University
Colby College
Colgate University
College of Charleston
College of the Holy Cross
College of William & Mary
College of Wooster
Colorado College
Columbia University
Connecticut College
Cornell University
Creighton University
CUNY Hunters College
Dartmouth College
Davidson College
Denison University
DePauw University
Dickinson College
Drexel University
Duke University
Duquesne University
Earlham College
East Carolina University
Elon University
Emerson College
Emory University
FIT
Florida State University
Fordham University

Franklin & Marshall College
Furman University
Geneva College
George Washington University
Georgetown University
Georgia Tech
Gettysburg College
Gonzaga University
Goucher College
Grinnell College
Grove City College
Guilford College
Gustavus Adolphus College
Hamilton College
Hampshire College
Hampton University
Hanover College
Harvard University
Harvey Mudd College
Haverford College
Hofstra University
Hollins University
Howard University
Idaho State University
Illinois State University
Illinois Wesleyan University
Indiana University
Iowa State University
Ithaca College
IUPUI
James Madison University
Johns Hopkins University
Juniata College
Kansas State
Kent State University
Kenyon College
Lafayette College
LaRoche College
Lawrence University
Lehigh University
Lewis & Clark College
Louisiana State University
Loyola College in Maryland
Loyola Marymount University
Loyola University Chicago
Loyola University New Orleans
Macalester College
Marlboro College
Marquette University
McGill University
Miami University of Ohio
Michigan State University
Middle Tennessee State
Middlebury College
Millsaps College
MIT
Montana State University
Mount Holyoke College
Muhlenberg College
New York University
North Carolina State
Northeastern University
Northern Arizona University
Northern Illinois University
Northwestern University
Oberlin College
Occidental College

Ohio State University
Ohio University
Ohio Wesleyan University
Old Dominion University
Penn State University
Pepperdine University
Pitzer College
Pomona College
Princeton University
Providence College
Purdue University
Reed College
Rensselaer Polytechnic Institute
Rhode Island School of Design
Rhodes College
Rice University
Rochester Institute of Technology
Rollins College
Rutgers University
San Diego State University
Santa Clara University
Sarah Lawrence College
Scripps College
Seattle University
Seton Hall University
Simmons College
Skidmore College
Slippery Rock
Smith College
Southern Methodist University
Southwestern University
Spelman College
St. Joseph's University Philladelphia
St. John's University
St. Louis University
St. Olaf College
Stanford University
Stetson University
Stony Brook University
Susquahanna University
Swarthmore College
Syracuse University
Temple University
Tennessee State University
Texas A & M University
Texas Christian University
Towson University
Trinity College Connecticut
Trinity University Texas
Truman State
Tufts University
Tulane University
UC Berkeley
UC Davis
UC Irvine
UC Riverside
UC San Diego
UC Santa Barbara
UC Santa Cruz
UCLA
Union College
University at Albany
University at Buffalo
University of Alabama
University of Arizona
University of Central Florida
University of Chicago

University of Colorado
University of Connecticut
University of Delaware
University of Denver
University of Florida
University of Georgia
University of Illinois
University of Iowa
University of Kansas
University of Kentucky
University of Maine
University of Maryland
University of Massachusetts
University of Miami
University of Michigan
University of Minnesota
University of Mississippi
University of Missouri
University of Nebraska
University of New Hampshire
University of North Carolina
University of Notre Dame
University of Oklahoma
University of Oregon
University of Pennsylvania
University of Pittsburgh
University of Puget Sound
University of Rhode Island
University of Richmond
University of Rochester
University of San Diego
University of San Francisco
University of South Carolina
University of South Dakota
University of South Florida
University of Southern California
University of Tennessee
University of Texas
University of Utah
University of Vermont
University of Virginia
University of Washington
University of Wisconsin
UNLV
Ursinus College
Valparaiso University
Vanderbilt University
Vassar College
Villanova University
Virginia Tech
Wake Forest University
Warren Wilson College
Washington and Lee University
Washington University in St. Louis
Wellesley College
Wesleyan University
West Point
West Virginia University
Wheaton College IL
Wheaton College MA
Whitman College
Wilkes University
Williams College
Xavier University
Yale University